The Business Owner's Guide to Profit

Ben Slater

This paperback edition was first published in 2017

First Published in Australia in 2017 by
'Systems For Business Press'
560 Hanel Street, East Albury,
NSW, 2640
www.systemsforbusinesspress.com

Typeset in (Open Sans, Helvetica)
Printed in China

The moral right of the authors has been asserted

IBSN – 978 0 646 97123 0

THIS BOOK IS DEDICATED TO MY FATHER DAVID FOR
TEACHING ME HOW TO PLAY THE GAME, MY BROTHER
DREW FOR TEACHING ME DRIVE AND MY MENTOR
LACHLAN CAMERON FOR TEACHING ME ABOUT LIFE
AND LEVERAGE

TABLE OF CONTENTS

PRELUDE

There was a boy born in the 4th century B.C in Athens.

He was born into a wealthy family and surrounded by the most influential people of his country.

The boy was extremely bright, and went through the first few years of his life excelling in gymnastics and mathematics. He was educated at a very high level, and gifted with a rare intellectual curiosity that drove him to seek a greater understanding of the world around him. It wasn't long before the boy surpassed his teachers in their fields, much to their dismay.

The young boy's thirst for knowledge was inspired by his father, who had always placed a high value on education. However, his father would never see the boy's journey unfold. At a very young age, the boy's father died of sudden causes. The pain of losing his father, the heroic figure in his life, catapulted his mission to further understand the 'nature of reality.'

His continued curiosity soon lead him to the introduction of his first mentor.

This mentor had previously been referred to as *'the wisest man in all of Greece,'* by the Oracle of Delphi, to which the mentor responded *"I am the wisest man alive, because I know that I know nothing."*

The boy cherished his relationship with his new mentor. He began to learn so much about the manner of dialogue and the systems for discovering philosophy, and 'true knowledge', or 'the logo's' as his mentor had called it. In the absence of his father, this mentor soon took shape as the boy's father figure.

In his early twenties the boy awoke to his brother Glaucon, with some terrible news. His mentor had been incarcerated by the city, and was to be tried in contempt of the court for violating the mind's of youth.

The mentor had the ability to deconstruct the thoughts of others through a powerful form of strategic questions and dialogue. He was known to be able to make the most self-righteous men in Greece look stupid, and consequently he had made many enemies.

These same enemies had instigated his incarceration.

His mentor was eventually found guilty by the court for 'corrupting the youth,' and was sentenced to death. The mentor was given the chance to recount for his sins, but instead he stood strong to his philosophical teachings, and preceded to drink the poison.

Having now lost two father figures in his early years, the boy had lost faith in his government. He had lost faith in his country, and it's politics. He soon left Greece and went to Egypt, seeking education on the mysteries in the school of Isis.

The boy spent many years in Egypt before returning to Greece. Upon his return, the boy-turned-man had acquired another mentor. This mentor had also been in Egypt, where they had shared the same ambition to study the mysteries of nature.

Over the course of the boy's life he had experienced a lifetime of trials and tribulations. He had confronted political systems, and had been held captive for his confrontations.

He witnessed multiple attempts at his second mentors life. To this day it is unknown if he survived.

After a lifetime of struggle, this young boy had grown into the man who would set up a school in Athens called 'The Academy.' By this time, he had become a great philosopher; he had synthesized his knowledge, and had started to share his wisdom with his students.

At the entrance to the school it read *"Let none who enter who are ignorant of geometry."*

Students came from near and far to study at 'The Academy', and to this day, the man has become one of the greatest intellectual leaders known to man.

The man I speak of in the story is Plato. His first mentor was Socrates, and his second mentor was Pythagoras.

Plato is responsible for more of our western thought than anyone in history. He is, quite literally, the most influential person in the world of philosophy today.

One of my favorite quotes from Plato is *"Those who tell stories, rule society."*

And it can be easily seen why Plato's mentors were so ruthlessly dismayed during their lifetimes – and even killed in Socrates case. Pythagoras too, faced attempted murder; and to this day it is unknown whether he survived, though none of his original writings are available.

All of Plato's original writings from that time are still available today.

Plato told stories through dialogue and allegory; Pythagoras and Socrates didn't. Plato became aware that his ideas were so confrontational to the mass of minds at the time that if he didn't present them in story, in an allegory, then he may face the same fate.

Plato was known to say, *"There is none more hated than he who speaks the truth."* I believe this is in reference to what he saw unfold with his mentors. It was only through the pain of death Plato was able to 'stand on the shoulders of the Giants' before him to create the most influential philosophic doctrines in the world today.

Many of which have greatly impacted this book.

Plato went on to mentor Aristotle and Aristotle then mentored Alexander the Great. From the line of thinkers and influencers you can see here – from Socrates and Pythagoras into Plato into Aristotle into Alexander the Great – these five individuals have had more of an impact on the development of the Western world than any other five people combined.

I tell you this story for two reasons. Firstly to show you the power of the mentor and student relationship, which is a theme, we will build on throughout this book. And secondly to illustrate that, the most powerful aspect of business is storytelling.

There's a powerful copywriting axiom – "Show, don't tell." We like to be shown, to some degree we like to keep the mystery alive. And we can also add this to another great axiom from the world of copywriting – "You need to enter the conversation that the prospect or the client is having in their mind."

There is no greater tool for Business than using these two great axioms and then creating a three term proportion by combining it with the philosophy of Plato...

"Those who tell stories rule society."

I like to think of it as something like this:

The mind is a castle. We get bombarded with 5,000 advertising and media messages every single day. So what do we do? We built a moat around our mind and we push all of these messages out.

We cannot physically maintain the level of energy required to process 5,000 messages per day.

It's hard enough maintaining the castle as it is. So we are beneficially designed to have cognitive bias towards these messages and to consciously and unconsciously reject marketing messages.

So... How do you get a message into the castle?

You use the Trojan horse.

The Trojan horse is story, and the mind is always open to story. Because you are not leading with what you want to tell, but rather leading with what you want to show.

And as the metaphor evolves, you can break out and run a muck.

THE TROJAN HORSE

In every chapter of this book, I have included a story, a study, or some evidence of what I'm saying to you. That's because I'm trying to show you and I'm not trying to tell you. I'm trying to help you come to the same realizations I've come to and I need to present it to you in a way you feel it.

There is a common misconception in Business that we have to hide behind a Logo. However I have seen the opposite to be exponentially more effective. The ultimate tool to storytelling in business is telling your whole story. Hold nothing back.

If you want your private past to be separate from your public present then you haven't owned your past, it's still baggage for you. And here's the kicker... You'll never share something with the world until you're grateful for it. And when you do it becomes fuel to your fire.

My entry into Entrepreneurship came in very unlikely origins... When I was 16 years old I watched my fathers Business decline and one of our cars get repossessed.

At the time I didn't understand how to respond. I asked why me? I asked why us? I asked why now?

I had just moved schools to a much larger school and none of my friends were going through these struggles at home. So I turned towards drugs and alcohol. Because often times the path of internal realisation is too painful so we turn to the outside.

Four years later I could barely go out in public without hallucinating. I was heavily medicated and so scared. I lost everything I thought was important to me. I suffered fear and pain in short moments to last a lifetime and it was the best thing that ever happened to me.

It was a rare baptism of fire that has led me into a rare Values System for someone my age and I couldn't be more grateful to have experienced it.

So you may ask, "How does Ben show like this?"

My success in business and in life is in direct correlation, not only the pain that I've been through but also my ability to synthesize that pain. My single greatest tool for doing that is telling my personal story with others and holding nothing back from you because I've got nothing to hide. There is nothing I cannot say or do in business, there's nothing I'm scared of saying anymore, and that's where my power is.

Why do "those who tell stories rule society?" Because when we tell other people's stories we connect and therefore we rise in Influence and Impact. And when we are Vulnerable enough to share our personal stories, we transcend all that keeps us limited. We become present, we become certain, we become enthusiastic, we unconditionally love ourselves, and we rise.

So... What is your personal power story? What have you transcended in your life? This even goes far beyond just business and marketing, you will hear me talk about the Hero's Journey and I will say, it's a goal of every person's life to share the gifts found in their struggles with their fellow man.

BUSINESS BREAKTHROUGH QUESTION – What is your Personal Power Story?

ACTION ITEM – Once you understand your personal power story, share it with the world. Post it on Facebook. Put it in your speeches, your sales presentations, your marketing and your profile. Remember your public present must not be separate from your private past.

ACTION ITEM – George Orwell once said, "A scrupulous writer, in every sentence that he writes, will ask himself at least four questions, thus: 1. What am I trying to say? 2. What Words will express it? 3. What image or idiom will make it clearer? 4. Is this image fresh enough to have an effect?" When you are reading develop a system to collect stories, to add into your marketing. Personally I mark the pages and transcribe them onto note cards, filing them into an organised system for use later on.

Read on...

PART 1: INTRODUCTIONS

THE ART AND SCIENCE OF BUSINESS…

On the 15th of April 1452, a boy was born in Florence. Born out of wedlock. His father was a wealthy notary in the city of Florence and his mother, a poor peasant.

Little is known of the first few years on the boy's life…. However it is known he spent the first five years of his life living in poor conditions with his mother. Then the boy moved to live with his father.

The relationship was troubled from the beginning because the son was a bastard. And at that time – for the wealthy and notary people – this was somewhat of an embarrassment. His father would later go on to marry another three times and have close to twelve siblings – all of whom, heirs to their fathers fortune.

It is said that the boy had an 'unquenchable curiosity' and a 'feverishly inventive imagination.'

One of his earlier memories did arise much later in his life, through the study of his prolific and personal notebooks.

Here is his account…

"Unable to resist my eager desire and wanting to see the great wealth of the various and strange shapes made by the formative nature and having wandering off some distance amongst gloomy rocks…

I came to the entrance of a great cavern, in front of which I stood some time, astonished and unaware of such a thing. Bending my back into an arch I rested my left hand on my knee I held my right hand over my down-cast and contracted eyebrows:

Often bending first one way and then the other, to see whether

I could discover anything inside, and this being forbidden by the deep darkness, and after having remained there for some time, two contrary emotions arose in me, fear and desire.

Fear of the threatening dark cavern and desire to see whether there were any marvellous things in it"

Versed in the areas of invention, painting, sculpting, architecture, science, music, mathematics, engineering, literature, anatomy, geology, astronomy, botany, writing, history, and cartography.

He is best known for his artistic presence and his scientific inventions. He synthesized these two complimentary opposites into the greater whole and it is because of this that Leonardo Da Vinci is one of the rare immortals that still influences the world from beyond the grave today.

The reason why I bring this up is that Da Vinci has informed – through a single quote – The framework on which this book rests.

Da Vinci once shared...

"My Four Principles For the Development of a Complete Mind.

1. Study the Science of Art.
2. Study the Art of Science.
3. Develop Your Senses... Especially Learn How to See.
4. Realize That Everything Connects to Everything Else."

What you are holding in your hands is a mind – an idea, a system you can use. It's a paradigm, a framework and a scaffold that can support your business as you build it to new heights.

It's a geometric structure you can plug your business into to double your net profits.

I call it the 'Systems for Business Philosophy.' And at the entrance to this school, let it be read,

"Let none enter who are ignorant of geometry."

Leonardo Da Vinci is believed by many to be the greatest creative genius that ever lived, but what most don't know is this is not solely due to his painting.

Da Vinci also mathematically and scientifically studied the proportions of the body. He dissected the body. He understood everything about the bones, the muscles, the tendons, the joints and the ligaments. He was a polymath.

Polymath – a person of wide-ranging knowledge or learning.

He understood nature scientifically so that, when it came time to become the artist, he used his system to produce the most beautiful and memorable pieces of art the world has ever seen.

In any area of study, there are two complementary opposite parts of the whole. This is what Da Vinci alluded to when he said, "study the science of art and study the art of science."

Study the left-brain. Study the right brain. Study the polarity present in all things.

For Da Vinci his art was his painting, his science was geometry and proportion...

And what's most exciting about 'Da Vinci's Four Principles...'

These same laws apply to your business.

In business the art is psychology.

The science is basic math and knowing your numbers.

"Business is Math and Psychology"

As a result this book you are holding in your hands presents you with a mathematic formula to improve the 'Lifetime Profit Value' of your clients... It also presents strategies founded in human behavioural psychology to improve the functions in your equation...

What is presented here is the Philosophy behind how to build a profitable business. And the word "philosophy" comes from two words in Ancient Greek. The first is "philo" meaning "love" and the second is "sophia" meaning "wisdom."

Philosophy is the word used to describe the 'love of wisdom.'

My question to you is; Do you want to go beyond merely playing on the surface in Business? Do you want to build a beautiful and influential structure?

Then you have to look at the individuals throughout history who had the greatest 'love for wisdom.' Because there is a direct correlation between this love and influence.

And what is business if not influence?

Throughout this book, I have told stories about Da Vinci, I have told stories about Plato, I will share stories about and quote from the greatest minds, myths and ideas who have ever informed us.

Would it surprise you to know these great thinkers applied systems to develop their concepts?

I am here to help you drastically improve the profitability of your business. So we start at the top and we go to the greatest minds, the greatest ideas that have ever lived, and we adapt them and use them in your business.

This book presents both sides. I'm giving you the math and I'm also giving you the psychology.

Which is why I'm writing this to you... My intention is to help you study the science of art and to help you to study the art of science.

Only through the synthesis of these two elements will you develop your businesses senses and learn how to see what's happening around you.

I have a firm belief than no one is smarter than anyone else, no one is more intuitive, more creative, more of a genius than anyone else. We all possess these qualities equality. So when I write, and when I teach, I respect you enough to treat you like a genius. I believe everyone is a genius when they love themselves enough to live through their highest values.

I want you to understand as you go through this book, I've decided to hold nothing back from you, so at times you may feel a little overwhelmed. Just know that overwhelm is a great thing because it means you are learning.

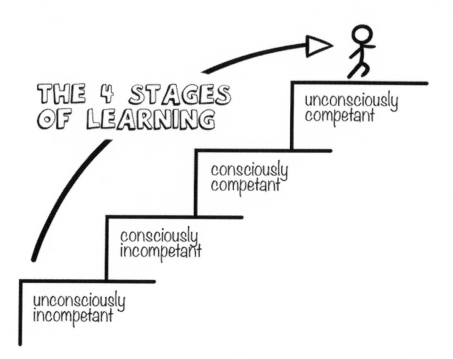

THE 4 STAGES OF LEARNING

unconsciously competant

consciously competant

consciously incompetant

unconsciously incompetant

The reason why I'm writing this book is so you don't have to spend years and years stuck in each stage of your journey like most people do. Too many people spend their whole lives living into such a small pixel of their potential.

There's no reason to stay stuck for any extended period of time in your mission.

As a Business Owner I want to congratulate you, because most never even make it this far. Think of all the people you talk to in your life. How many people are still stuck in victim mentality?

Victor Frankl once said, "Between stimulus and response there is a space, and within that space lies our power to choose our response, and within our response lies our ultimate growth and freedom.'

What differentiates us as business owners, is that we heard a stimulus deep inside, an inner voice and an irrationally passionate desire to become something more. We felt the space more intensely, we entered into the pain, and we have chosen the response that serves our ultimate growth and freedom.

This choice is never easy, though for me, the path of entrepreneurship, of paving our own way, is the most efficient path to long term positive impact in the world.

Winston Churchill said, "To each there comes in their lifetime a special moment when they are figuratively tapped on the shoulder and offered the chance to do a very special thing, unique to them and fitted to their talents. What a tragedy if that moment finds them unprepared or unqualified for what could have been their finest hour"

As an entrepreneur, you've been trusted. You were trusted to be strong enough to push through your challenges, and lead all those behind you. There is no reason why each day shouldn't involve some of your finest hours.

The secret is to know exactly where you are right now, then chart your course. Show gratitude and find your self image. Seek what you need that you don't have, and then take huge amounts of daily action.

THE AGE OF INFORMATION

No longer are the wealthiest amongst us rising through commodities and the coat tails of the titans of industry.

The rising millionaires are the entrepreneurs who have found a way to increase the efficiency and speed of information. The rising millionaires are those who have facilitated breakthroughs in knowledge. The rising millionaires are those who have encouraged the transcendence of all that keeps us disconnected.

The businesses that are dominating their industries hold no stock. The entrepreneurs who are leading the pack are those who have prioritized ideas, systems and the development of intellectual property over money.

We are in the information economy and it's time for us all to enter more fully into it. If your goal is to make more profit. There is nothing more profitable than the seeking and selling of knowledge.

I bring this up because most business owners have their desired outcomes flipped in reverse... They limit their knowledge and sell their time to make money. If you want to climb the corporate ladder and you are willing to wait 30 years for your payoff maybe this will work for you.

THE MASSES

ꩰꩰꩰꩰ → $ Money > ⏲ Time > φ Knowledge

But I'm guessing it's not. So why follow the same corporations who would love to enslave us to those tiny cubicles...

Personally... I have always followed the premise, 'create your own system or be enslaved by another man's...'

Here's the best way I have found.

Spend your time maximizing your knowledge and then selling your Intellectual Property, Systems and Ideas for Money...

THE MASTER

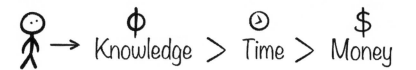

In this book I will deal primarily with the packaging, marketing and selling of your Intellectual Property and Knowledge Based Systems. Because when done correctly you will never have to pay to store them, you can run a business from anywhere in the world and the smarter you become the more money you will make.

You can become an expert in your chosen field... You can rise in influence and impact as you build a business around your purpose, your vision and your mission...

Into 2017 and beyond the old conventional notions of business are dead and those who hang on too tight to the bricks and mortar may never find how empowered they could have become.

All this considered... Your success within the age of information isn't solely contained in the seeking of knowledge... As Tony Robbins once said, "Knowledge without action is insanity."

As i mentioned earlier, there are two complementary opposite parts of the whole. And to create anything in business you need to blend yin and yang, or knowledge and action. At the end of the day, your business is about these two things only, Knowledge and Action – Knowledge of marketing and the actions you need to take to get the leads; knowledge of how to make your sales and the intrinsic drive to get up and action your process everyday; Knowledge of how to deliver the right services and the actions you need to take to make sure it's all functioning smoothly.

It's all knowledge and action. Business Growth takes it clearest and most simple picture from a consistent oscillation between knowledge and action, and the one who bounces fastest wins.

THE HERO'S JOURNEY

What do Homer's Iliad, Harry Potter, The Bible, Lord of the Rings, The Story of Siddhartha Buddha, Star Wars, Game of Thrones and most Disney movies have in common?

Besides from being the highest grossing and most influential storylines of all time... These great Myths also have a common storyline. They intentionally follow the same ark. And it's a familiar pattern originally popularised and brought to mass appeal by Joseph Campbell through his PBS series titled *'The Power of Myth'* in 1988.

On closer inspection one will find this pattern is nothing new and has been embedded in the Human Psyche for as far back as history will allow us to see.

In modern times the use of this pattern is by no means an accident. George Lucas consulted with Campbell and intentionally followed the pattern in the development of his Stars Wars franchise. Which was recently sold to Disney for over 4 Billion Dollars.

The reason we love these stories so much goes so far beyond intellectual entertainment. These stories match our spiritual nature, we see our struggles inside them; we enter into these movies, we feel the voids, we share their values... We live to tread the hero path.

What's most exciting? In life and business we can use this pattern to tap into our potential.

Joseph Campbell was an American Mythologist who studied all

of the great myths from around the world – the Egyptian myths, the Hindu-Indian myths, the Upanishads, the Bhagavad Gita, the Mayan myths, Australian myths and myths from all great indigenous cultures from every corner of the world.

What Campbell found was there was an archetypal pattern that runs through them all. He called it 'The Hero's Journey'.

This raises some of the most important questions I have ever encountered about the nature of human consciousness and the dynamics of growth.

How is it possible that from each corner of the globe the greatest teachers from times past, those whose stories became imbedded in our lives were using the same ark for their stories?

Here's what Joseph Campbell had to say about 'The Hero's Journey;'

> *"Furthermore, We have not even to risk the adventure alone, for the heroes of all time have gone before us — the labyrinth is thoroughly known. We have only to follow the thread of the hero path, and where we had thought to find an abomination, we shall find a god; where we had thought to slay another, we shall slay ourselves; where we had thought to travel outward, we shall come to the centre of our own existence. And where we had thought to be alone, we shall be with all the world"*

Campbell discovered 17 stages in the development of the Human Psyche.

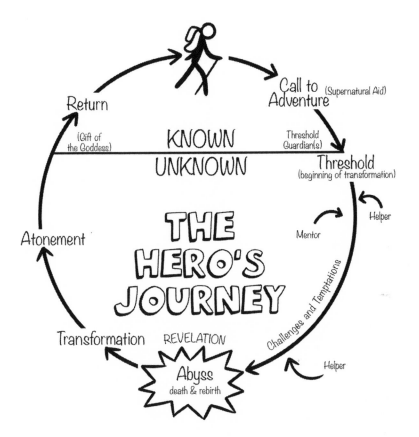

Firstly we get a call to adventure. Then, we cross from the known world into the unknown world – or from the conscious to the unconscious mind. We experience many challenges and temptations there and we meet a mentor.

Then, we enter the void. We have something happen to us, something traumatic. Every single myth that follows the Hero's Path has this great fight with the void.

I'm sure you can visualise your own voids...

Luke Skywalker had his first meeting with Darth Vader, Jon Snow went to the wall, Jesus was hung on the cross, and Aladdin loses the power of the genie.

Your mentor then puts their hand into the void and pulls you out... And as you come up out of the void, you start to integrate your personality. You begin the road to return. You have your trials and tribulations, the transformation and atonement.

But then, you come to the most important stage of the journey. Crossing back from the unknown world into the known world.

And during the final stages, you return with the boon. And by returning with the boon you bestow your gifts upon your fellow man and you become a master of the two worlds.

You share your hard won lessons and triumphs with your world, in the form of an integrated personality, Holy Grail or victory and you become the Hero.

If we're looking at this really basically, someone ventures out into the unknown, they meet a mentor, they have an issue, they overcome that issue, and then they share the knowledge of what they've overcome. They become the mentor with value to add to the world.

What most people don't realise is the reason why this story line is embedded amongst Myths from all cultures is because we all follow these same patterns in our lives. It's part of the Human Experience. The path of growth and development in any endeavour follows the Hero's Journey. How amazing is that?

There is an underlying background. A container that is supporting your growth.

Think about it... This is exactly what business is. This is what entrepreneurship is all about. It's about venturing onto a path unknown, facing challenges and temptations, overcoming voids, finding mentors and sharing value.

It's about sharing knowledge.

Leo Tolstoy once said, "Knowledge is the light of life and the darkness cannot extinguish it." He said this because the true goal of the Hero's Journey is to bring to light and flame human consciousness and if we tap into this, if we can become conscious members of the Hero's Journey, we can known where to tread, who to serve and how to transcend all that keeps us limited in life and business.

Unfortunately most people don't realize they are in the midst of their Hero's Journey and therefore they are wearing a blindfold, wandering around in the dark of the Labyrinth.

But what if as Joseph Campbell said, *"the labyrinth is thoroughly known."*

I have found this to be true over and over again in my life.

Let me mention, we are far more similar than our secular education would have us believe. There are patterns, in the evolution of Human Consciousness and a few Universal Laws that rule over this realm.

My mentor Lachlan once described these laws to me as huge waves. We could swim out there and get tossed under, throw aside, and maybe even drown. Or we could grab a surfboard, enter into the process of learning, and eventually have the time of our lives.

Socrates said, *"the highest form of learning is teaching."* He said this because you only ever synthesize your learning completely once you share the boon with others; you only integrate the unconscious and the conscious mind by returning with the boon and bestowing your gifts upon your fellow man.

What I've noticed about Entrepreneurs is too often we fall to our fears. And... It happens to me all the time too, more than most.

You're right at the edge of crossing back into the known world to share your gifts and you just can't seem to push through. And it's perfectly understandable because until now you haven't known the science, you didn't know the symbols, you didn't know how to follow the path.

But as the Greek sage Hermes said, *"Once you step foot on this path, you see it everywhere."*

That fear that you feel – *"Oh, am I allowed to step on the stage and share my story? Am I allowed to share this? Am I allowed to do that?"*

With an understanding of the Hero's Journey, you realise, *"Who am I not to?"*

Because when you share your boon, when you cross back into the known world, you enter into someone else's Hero's Journey when they need it most. This is the completion of the cycle because you become the mentor.

Do you remember what it meant, when your mentor confronted their fears to help you? Think about where you would be without them and the fear subsides.

With this in mind, the smartest thing you can do in business is progressively master every aspect of yourself, and then sell that information back to others.

How to do that?

Firstly you need to understand, what it's really worth to someone to transcend his or her issues in the areas of health, wealth or relationships?

What we're talking about here is life changing transformational value?

It's priceless...

When you start to play in this realm in your business, when you start to leverage your successes, your failures and you sell this back to others. This is how you can drastically increase your average dollar sale and move into higher-ticket products and services.

Many people talk about 'High-Ticket Sales...' But I've never heard anyone talk about how you do it. How you sell Higher Ticket items is by owning yourself, owning your mindset and developing yourself personally. Because, when you do, you command more value. And only then will you feel worthy of becoming more.

Think about your life right now. Have a look at your life. What I've given you here is a pattern you can follow... What have you overcome? Where are you empowered? Where do you have specific and valuable knowledge as a result of your challenges? Is it health? Are you socially empowered? Are you empowered with family dynamics? Is it personal finance? Is it career and business? Is it intellectually? Is it spiritually? Is it intimately and sexually?

BUSINESS BREAKTHROUGH QUESTION – "Where are you uniquely empowered? Can you sell this information back to others?"

You have it! Everyone does, but at times we don't allow ourselves to step into it.

And the best thing about this is once we start to teach it, then we really master the process and our learning accelerates at an unprecedented rate. By tapping into this pattern, you step into your greatness and your role of the mentor. You become more empowered. And you can make far more value per average sale than you're making right now.

This is a great secret of Carl Jung's Depth Psychology. There is an underlying background, an underlying force that's supporting you and helping you to get to where you want to go. You can become conscious in it. You can step into it. You can become a member of it, which is so beautiful.

As you're moving forwards I would love to invite you to think more about this, because it's a huge untapped area of growth for entrepreneurs.

For each cycle of the Hero's Journey that you own, and transcend you step up to a higher level – a higher quantum of your awareness. Which means you start to make a lot more money. The biggest mistake – as I said earlier – is that entrepreneurs have these fears. "Oh, no, I've got to hang on to my idea! I've got to hang on to my business and the way that it is!"

You limit yourself when you do that. You could think of the Hero's Journey as an Oscillation between destruction and exhibition of the Ego. So if you're holding onto your Ego too tight you will die never knowing what an amazing person you might have become.

My advice is as you move through the Hero's Journey. You don't have to slow down you have to calm down.

You can apply the speed of implementation. Do not stop. Burn things to the ground if you have to just never stop moving forwards. Never assume where you're moving to isn't a more empowered place than where you've already been. If you're tapping into your psyche, if you're seeking the right knowledge and taking action, it always is.

When you're learning you're always becoming more empowered, but at times you just can't see it. You're unconscious to all the areas you're becoming empowered in. Therefore, you limit yourself and you limit everyone around you.

The key is to show gratitude for how far you've come and then if you want to increase the average dollar sale, could you set this intention from that space? Set the intention you want to increase your average dollar sale and increase it dramatically. Wait to see what comes your way and respond.

I moved from selling $20.00 how-to handstand programs to $5,000 programs to $36,000 business coaching programs within the space of twenty-four months. I was able to do this because I tapped into the mentor and student relationship. I became a conscious member of the Hero's Journey and I decoded every single event, person, place and circumstance along the path. I knew what it meant and how to respond. It therefore enabled me to fast track my growth because what I saw in others, I could see in myself. I wasn't too humble or too arrogant to believe the mentor wasn't the student and the voids, trials and tribulations were anything permanent.

We are living in an ocean of motion. Could you learn how to surf?

BUSINESS BREAKTHROUGH QUESTION – What have you

transcended in your life? Could you become the mentor to those still in your struggle?

ACTION ITEM – "When the student is ready the mentor will appear." If you are in a void in any of the 7 areas of life... Affirm your position and seek the mentor. What you are asking for will be provided. Often not in the way we expect.

ACTION ITEM – Become conscious in the great cycle. Read 'The Power of Myth' and 'The Hero's Journey'

This is one of the greatest areas of study in Personal Development – Because, once you learn how to decode mythology, you begin to see it within your own life. And because these great myths were coming from what Carl Jung called the 'collective unconscious' – the part of our mind that is ultimately connected and not bound in time and space – the human psyche, the human soul. We can tap into it to find out where we should head. If you're open this will elevate your life to a completely new level of awareness and understanding.

One of the biggest flaws I see in the mindset of the masses is they are unaware their current level of thinking has created every problem they are facing. As a result they don't spend anywhere near enough time seeking new knowledge, and they relegate themselves to action the same ideas, on the same linear levels of thinking.

When I look at business. I see a continuous cycle of problem solving and a development of consciousness we are all accelerating through together. It's all about the acquisition of knowledge. And to acquire any knowledge we have to enter into the unknown, the yin - the unconscious.

When we start coming out of the unconscious and we enter back into the known world, it's all about the yang – It's all about ego and action.

The only way to truly succeed in business is through a consistent and conscious oscillation between the diminishment and exhibition of your ego.

This is why Socrates said; *'I am the wisest man alive because I know that I know nothing.'*

To learn something new you have to unlearn something old. And this is what most people fear. They fear what they might discover, and it makes them feel out of control. When in reality this is the only way to push through your self-limiting beliefs.

Remember earlier Da Vinci spoke of his moment at the entrance to the great cavern, when two contrary emotions arose, fear and desire. Any desire to learn or grow will accompany a fear. It's only through making the fear conscious do we experience the world of our desires.

When you enter into the cavern, the unknown... You have to come back out with your newfound knowledge or you will forever stay stuck in the cavern never completing anything.

By understanding the Hero's Journey you will see that, to seek knowledge without action is a very polarized way of living and one that will never see you get to where you want to go.

I've been guilty of this in the past and will continue to be in the future; it's been one of the biggest issues for me in business.

My brother Drew used to ask me a fantastic question – *"What is it we need that we don't have right now? What is the knowledge we need that we don't have?"* You could even say, *"What are the actions we're not taking that we need to be taking right now?"*

If you are constantly asking that question every day, every hour, every minute – "What do I need that I don't have?" – And you are ruthlessly chasing those things. And then you are implementing those things once you find them.

This is how you can build a successful business in a short amount of time. It's quite simple really.

So many people lie to themselves and pretend they have all the knowledge they need? From my perspective, it's mostly a fear of incoming, and feeling unworthy of growth. Those who exhibit the most arrogant ego are often the ones who feel the most scared inside. They fear the unknown.

Drew and I were lucky in that we had each other to offer support as we were ruthlessly chasing these things we didn't yet understand. But we were also really honest; which is why I have spent over $175,000 on my non-secular education in the past few years.

It was because I knew there were elements I didn't yet understand about business and I knew I could pay someone a measly sum of money compared to the return I could make. I was seeking mentors and as a result I accelerated the time taken to move through my Hero's Journey.

I will make multiples from the information I have invested in because I sought resources based off a simple question. From the very beginning of any business I'm now involved in. I know how to generate a lead; I know how to close a sale; and I know how to deliver online automated products, information products, events and seminars; I know how to upsell from events, I know how to get referrals, I know how to optimise and improve the Lifetime Value of a Client.

I had to pay for each of these pieces of the puzzle, handsomely and individually, and I had to put this puzzle together myself. It took me years to be able to present this system to you, but something to understand about me...

I dedicate my life to the acquisition and application of knowledge.

Every single weekend, I was in seminars. Every single minute of every single day, I wasn't going out partying. I was sitting there, reading books. I've got a thousand books in my library and I read them every day because I am ruthlessly chasing the things I don't yet understand.

And much of this comes down to psychology. I need to understand why I'm not taking action. What are the blockages? What is holding me back from taking action? I completed a Nuero-Linguistic Programming course. I'm trained in hypnosis, and I've done much of Dr John Demartini's work on human behaviour.

What I've discovered is, you can have all the knowledge in the world, and that's great. But, if you don't take action, you're no better than where you started. There are many academics, intellectuals and people who present fantastic ideas but they struggle to take the right actions, the entrepreneurial actions.

We only have to compare Nikola Tesla and Thomas Edison and look at the impact they both had in the world to see how this can play out. Nikola Tesla was a brilliant man – far more creative than Thomas Edison. He had some inventions that would still blow the world away if they were to be released.

Thomas Edison, although he may not have been as great an inventor – which sounds ridiculous, to say – He was far more entrepreneurial. He was taking the right actions – the actions designed around getting his products and services out into the world for profit.

Nikola Tesla was just creating concepts and ideas. He was a creative genius and he died poor. Had he changed the way he was taking action, had he been more entrepreneurial with what he was doing, I think the world would be a very different place right now. We may be transferring energy wirelessly. We'd be riding more serious waves of technology.

Can you imagine this?

The Greek Philosophers called knowledge the "Logos" and they termed the seeking of knowledge as another word for god. They believed that the rational striving for knowledge was the closest we would ever come to knowing god.

I too believe the universe is a feedback mechanism designed to learn about itself and it's seeking a synthesis of knowledge and action at all times. When you jump into this sphere, when you start seeking knowledge and becoming your own creative, when you start adding your unique ideas with other people's unique ideas.

As Isaac Newton said, you "stand on the shoulders of giants" to achieve creativity.

This is how you develop your intellectual property and it's not outside of you.

And this is what spirituality has come to mean to me.

By blending yin and yang physically through sex we create our children.

By blending yin and yang mentally and physically through knowledge and action we create wondrous ideas, supports, structure and scaffolds.

I have come to believe that entrepreneurship is the most closely aligned study to personal spirituality.

There is something amazing about the seeking of knowledge. I am often faced with a problem and I walk up to my library and I ask for a solution to my problem. I am drawn to a certain book I pick it up and start reading. I am often brought to tears of gratitude because there is my solution to my problem on the page right in front of me.

How can we experience these moments in our lives and not come into the realisation that the world is far more beautiful than we ever imagined.

These are the greatest moments in life. Synchronicities.

The experience of knowing within your heart Da Vinci's 4th Principle for the development of a complete mind... **"That Everything Connects to Everything Else."**

WHERE TO ALIGN YOUR INTELLECTUAL PROPERTY?

Socrates said, "To know thyself is the beginning of all wisdom." And I believe Socrates spoke of our personal values in this statement. When your life is aligned to your highest values, you no longer need to be motivated. You are intrinsically inspired from within. No one needs to remind you to do anything. You just do it.

Everyone has this potential in his or her life. But too often we subordinate our values system to others. I recommend you build a business around what's truly most important to you, structure it around knowledge and then get paid to seek this knowledge you would love to master.

Jean de La Fontaine once said, "Man is so made that when anything fires his soul, impossibilities vanish."

What's the thing that fires your soul? For me, it's human behaviour, entrepreneurship and how universal laws affect consciousness. I teach these principles in my Personal Development and Consulting Businesses. It was intentional to create two separate businesses because I feel I can be of more service to others and myself this way.

The soul directs the mind, which directs the body... You will never love a business that is not aligned to your purpose. And it's simply smoother. Whenever my life is aligned to my highest values I never find myself at a loss for action.

I get paid to learn about the things I'm fiercely interested in and then teach this knowledge to others, which is the highest form of my learning. Because I am doing this at such a rapid rate, the prices of my products and services have increased drastically over the past few years. My earning capacity would be in the top 0.0001 percent of the population for someone my age. At no stage is this going to change because I'm not going to stop learning and teaching.

What I'm saying to you right now, it's not outside of you. I'm not here on some pedestal. I'm not doing anything that's so uniquely challenging you couldn't do it, too. It's literally the most inspired thing anyone can do with his or her life.

Find out what's truly meaningful to you, study it, and then teach it to others. If you can't inspire yourself to do that, you may be lying to yourself about what's really important to you. With a small shift in strategy and some personal permission to do what you want, you will step into your greatness.

There was once a king of Argos, in Greece called Acrisius. The Oracle of Delphi had foretold the King; his grandson would kill him in an accident.

Confused because at the time, he had no grandchildren, though he had a beautiful daughter, Danae. The king feared for his own life so he chose to lock up his daughter and keep her away from any sort of relationship with any man.

He locked her up in a tower, reaching into the heavens. And one day the gods – in particular Zeus, heard Danae's weeping prayers.

Zeus took notice of her beauty and fell in love with the young Danae.

It is said, he travelled down in the night and, through a golden shower, permeated the walls and impregnated the young beauty.

Nine months later, Perseus was born. A demi-god – half-man, half-god.

As Acrisius came to realize what had transpired, he thought about killing them both, though he feared Zeus' wrath so he sent them out into the ocean. Destined to float far away.

They went a few days without food until eventually they ended up on the Greek island of Polydektes.

On the island, they came to know the king of Polydektes. This man was a cruel and ruthless tyrant. Though constantly in awe of her beauty this king wanted Danae to be his wife.

At this stage Perseus was developing into a very strong and capable young man. The king knew he would consistently protect his mother. So, he devised a plan to trick Perseus into a trap likely to impose his death.

On a drunken night in the palace, Acrisius challenged Perseus to bring him the head of Medusa the Gorgon. An impossible task as medusa was a gorgon with poisonous snakes for hair and her gaze could turn any man into stone.

Perseus self-righteously accepted the task. And as he was leaving through the gates, he ran into the gods, Hermes and Athena. He asked them for their help and they gave him a pair of winged sandals, an invisible cap, a sword, and a mirrored shield.

As Perseus went into the fight with Medusa, he found himself in a very sticky situation.

However on listening to the knowledge from Hermes, Perseus used the mirrored shield to reflect the gaze of Medusa. Only once he had reflected her gaze with the mirrored shield could Perseus slay the gorgon and rise up through his winged sandals...

Upon eventually returning to Civilisation Perseus was known to throw a discus in competition and Kill his Grandfather Acrisius as he watched on in the stands...

The reason I tell this story is because this is what entrepreneurship is really about. It's perceived to be a physical war but really it's all mindset. It has been said that 'our deepest fears are like dragons guarding our deepest treasure.'

In your business it's only once you reflect your gaze back inside do you slay these gorgons and you rise.

Medusa represents the great unknown. The unconscious void we must all overcome if we want to succeed in business. Hermes is the wise and intuitive higher mind, guiding you to the right book at your shelf. Only when you tune into your intuition will your true path be revealed.

Business is a mental game. It's not a physical war. It's not really Perseus fighting Medusa.

It's you fighting yourself.

Business is 80% mindset and 20% strategy and tactics.

Once you have won your internal war, the smartest thing you can do is to confront your fears and sell this knowledge back to others. Own these conflicting and contrasting elements within your business and sell this back to the person you once were.

If you perform a few cycles you will become a very financially empowered individual.

And on Acrisius... When you choose the wrong response to your fears you will undoubtedly bring those fears upon yourself.

I will show considerable evidence throughout the book that; the fears of mankind are what keep everyone small. Your fears about not feeling good enough to share your information with the world are not relevant to me because, if you're having a fear, your fear is either coming from one or two areas. You don't feel like you have enough information or you don't know how to inspire yourself to take action.

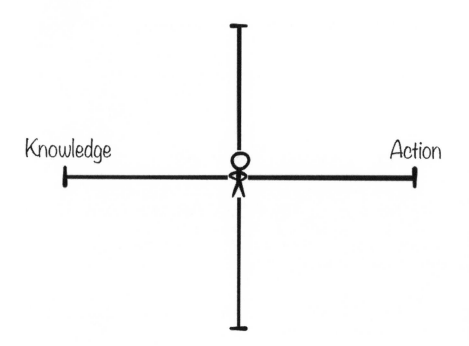

Put a plan in place to acquire all the knowledge you need. Tune into yourself, be vulnerable and honest, and ask for what you need. I have found this stimulus is always provided, just never in the way we imagine.

And remember this... **Self worth and knowledge come hand in hand, the more you understand about your nature, the faster you will rise through the octaves of life.**

This is the path. You seek it, you master it and then you teach it.

BUSINESS BREAKTHROUGH QUESTION - Where are you uniquely empowered? What special challenge, void, fight, trial or tribulation, have you overcome? What would it be worth to someone going through this same struggle to have access to your System?

WHAT IS the Average Lifetime Value of a Client? And How Do You Find it?

One of the biggest mistakes to make in life and business is to look externally before you have reaped your internal goldmine. As Steven Covey said, 'the private victory, must always proceed the public.' Now Steven was talking about mindset, and successful habits... And it's easy to cry 'irrelevance' here.

However the best way to improve your profit is to understand your basic numbers and then master their behavioural psychology.

Business is Maths and Psychology...

In this Chapter, we're dealing specifically with the mathematics, which may not be your strong point, but it's extremely important for you to have grounding in this before we venture into the psychology so you understand exactly where you are and exactly where you are going through the implementation of this system.

If you don't get this, you are building the rest of your scaffold on a shaky foundation.

According to Forbes Magazine... 50% of small businesses fail within the first 18 months, and 95% of small businesses fail within the first 10 Years.

After coaching hundreds of business owners and hopeful individuals over the past few years, I've found 8 Factors that define one's ability to crack it into the 5% and build a wildly profitable business.

This system I originally intellectualised through my readings and attendance at seminars. It was originally something I build for myself... And how I really mastered it was in the experiential learning's that were to come from applying it.

It becomes important to mention how to get the most out of this book. By simply reading this book you may consume some of the information, with some hope to implement it into the future...

However if you experience the exercises in this book, you will have a much broader perspective by which to apply it to your business and this will be worth thousands of dollars in increased income for you in the next few months if you truly apply yourself.

After and during each chapter I have included some relevant questions, exercises and action Items to complete. The book is intended for you to write in it, and create your own version of the system that provides you with a measurable return. So I ask that you don't sell yourself short in the application of this book.

The Average Lifetime Profit Value of a Client Calculation is a mathematical system that ignores accounting numbers and focuses firstly on income and then profit generation metrics in your business.

In a basic way it says. *If you were to bring in one client to your business tomorrow, on average how much Profit would that make you?*

This one figure and how to increase it is by far the most profound understanding of how to grow your business, and therefore how to increase your personal wealth.

This system, will drill down to the ONLY stats you need to measure and increase to Geometrically Grow Your Business.

And the most amazing thing about all this is there are only 8 of these Profit Maximisers...

How much more simple does it make it when you only have 8 things to focus on?

And here's where it gets really exciting; If you can improve these metrics by 10% each you will be introduced to what Albert Einstein called *'the 8th wonder of the World.'* **The Exponential Power of Compound Interest.**

So the 8 Metrics You Should Be Intensely Focussed On...

1. Lead Generation
2. Sales Closing Percentages On These Leads %
3. Average $ Sale
4. Profit Margins %
5. Average Purchases Per Year
6. Average Years Client Stays
7. Number of Referrals / Client / Year
8. Closing Percentages on Referrals %

If you can choose the strategies that suit you, follow the steps, I will outline and aim to just increase each metric by just 10%. How would your life and business change?

You will see in a moment, by making a few simple shifts you will double the Net Profits in your business.

And this is what the Lifetime Value Calculation is all about...

Finding and applying the appropriate vectors of leverage, 'the small hinges to shift the big doors.'

Before you start working through this book; it becomes important, if you don't know the Lifetime Profit Value of Your Clients, you need to go and work it out right now.

This may take some creative problem solving, but I guarantee you, you will get so much more out of this book if you do this before you move on.

It's a very enlightening process and as I said earlier, this is single most important metric you need to understand in your business.

Too many businesses get caught up in the accounting... 'Facts and figures' when in reality accounting is closer to creative writing than the pure and simple math in this book.

It is easy to think, all you need to do is to focus on the Current Assets, Liabilities and Balance Sheets. However, there are hidden profits sitting in front of you right now if you choose to mine your assets.

If you do the work this book will show you how.

EXERCISE 1 - WORK OUT YOUR AVERAGE LIFETIME PROFIT VALUE CALCULATION

A	PM # 1 - MONTHLY LEADS
B	ANNUAL LEADS (A X 12)
C	PM # 2 - SALES CONVERSION RATE (%)
D	NEW CLIENTS ANNUALLY (B X C)
E	PM # 3 - AVERAGE $ SALE
F	PM # 4 - PROFIT MARGIN
G	PROFIT PER SALE (E x F)
H	PM # 5 - AVERAGE PURCHASES / YEAR
I	PROFIT / YEAR (G X H)
J	PM # 6 - AVERAGE YEARS CLIENT STAYS
K	LIFETIME PROFIT VALUE OF EACH CLIENT (I X J)
L	LIFETIME PROFIT VALUE OF ALL CLIENT (D X K)
M	PM # 7 - NUMBER OF REFERRALS / CLIENT / YEAR
N	PM # 8 - REFERRAL CONVERSION RATE (%)
O	NUMBER OF CONVERTED REFERRALS / CLIENT / YEAR
P	NUMBER OF REFERRALS DURING LIFETIME (J X O)
Q	LIFETIME PROFIT FROM REFERRALS (K X P)
R	TOTAL LIFETIME PROFIT VALUE OF EACH CLIENT (K + Q)
S	TOTAL LIFETIME PROFIT VALUE FOR ALL NEW CLIENTS (R X D)

SYSTEMS for BUSINESS

I have included some online resources for this book. You can download your Average Lifetime Value of a Customer Template there; I have also included a quick 5 minute video to show you how to work out the Lifetime Value Calculation.

www.thesystemsforbusiness.com/lifetimevalue

WHAT WOULD HAPPEN IF YOU INCREASED THESE 8 METRICS BY 10% IN YOUR BUSINESS?

Let's jump into the hypothetical example below to further illustrate these powers for you; In this Hypothetical Example this Business is currently generating;

A - Monthly Leads – 100	A - Monthly Leads – 110
C - Sales Conversion - 20%	C - Sales Conversion - 22%
E - Average $ Sale - $997.00	E - Average $ Sale - $1096.70
F - Profit Margins - 30% VS	F - Profit Margins - 33%
H - Average Purchases / YEAR - 2.5	H - Average Purchases / YEAR - 2.75
J - Years Client Stays - 1.8	J - Years Client Stays - 1.98
M - Number of Referrals / Year - 1.5	M - Number of Referrals / Year - 1.65
N - Referral Conversion Rate - 30%	N - Referral Conversion Rate - 33%

What i've done on the following page is simply increase the 8 key profit maximisers in the business by 10% and... and the profits in the business have risen from $584,680.68 to $1, 189,227.14.

By increasing 8 metrics in your business by 10% you more than double the net profits in your business.

What happens when you add 10% to the 8 profit maximisers?

		100%	110%
A	PM # 1 - MONTHLY LEADS	100	110
B	ANNUAL LEADS (A X 12)	1200	1320
C	PM # 2 - SALES CONVERSION RATE (%)	20%	22%
D	NEW CLIENTS ANNUALLY (B X C)	240	290.4
E	PM # 3 - AVERAGE $ SALE	$997.00	$1,096.70
F	PM # 4 - PROFIT MARGIN	30%	33%
G	PROFIT PER SALE (E x F)	$299.10	$361.91
H	PM # 5 - AVERAGE PURCHASES / YEAR	2.5	2.75
i	PROFIT / YEAR (G X H)	$747.75	$995.26
J	PM # 6 - AVERAGE YEARS CLIENT STAYS	1.8	1.98
K	LIFETIME PROFIT VALUE OF EACH CLIENT (I X J)	$1,345.95	$1,970.61
L	LIFETIME PROFIT VALUE OF ALL CLIENT (D X K)	$323,028.00	$572,263.81
M	PM # 7 - NUMBER OF REFERRALS / CLIENT / YEAR	1.5	1.65
N	PM # 8 - REFERRAL CONVERSION RATE (%)	30%	33%
O	NUMBER OF CONVERTED REFERRALS / CLIENT / YEAR	0.45	0.5445
P	NUMBER OF REFERRALS DURING LIFETIME (J X O)	0.81	1.07811
Q	LIFETIME PROFIT FROM REFERRALS (K X P)	$1,090.22	$2,124.53
R	TOTAL LIFETIME PROFIT VALUE OF EACH CLIENT (K + Q)	$2,436.17	$4,095.13
S	TOTAL LIFETIME PROFIT VALUE FOR ALL NEW CLIENTS (R X D)	$584,680.68	$1,189,227.14

SYSTEMS for BUSINESS

EXERCISE 2 – Experience it for yourself... ADD 10% TO YOUR KEY METRICS

S3 SYSTEMS for BUSINESS

		100%	110%
A	PM # 1 - MONTHLY LEADS		
B	ANNUAL LEADS (A X 12)		
C	PM # 2 - SALES CONVERSION RATE (%)		
D	NEW CLIENTS ANNUALLY (B X C)		
E	PM # 3 - AVERAGE $ SALE		
F	PM # 4 - PROFIT MARGIN		
G	PROFIT PER SALE (E x F)		
H	PM # 5 - AVERAGE PURCHASES / YEAR		
I	PROFIT / YEAR (G X H)		
J	PM # 6 - AVERAGE YEARS CLIENT STAYS		
K	LIFETIME PROFIT VALUE OF EACH CLIENT (I X J)		
L	LIFETIME PROFIT VALUE OF ALL CLIENT (D X K)		
M	PM # 7 - NUMBER OF REFERRALS / CLIENT / YEAR		
N	PM # 8 - REFERRAL CONVERSION RATE (%)		
O	NUMBER OF CONVERTED REFERRALS / CLIENT / YEAR		
P	NUMBER OF REFERRALS DURING LIFETIME (J X O)		
Q	LIFETIME PROFIT FROM REFERRALS (K X P)		
R	TOTAL LIFETIME PROFIT VALUE OF EACH CLIENT (K + Q)		
S	TOTAL LIFETIME PROFIT VALUE FOR ALL NEW CLIENTS (R X D)		

Seneca said, "When a ship doesn't know which harbour it is aiming, no wind is the right wind," and now that you know where we're heading together; you just have to add 10% to your key metrics over the next 24 months. (I think you can do way more... But don't tell the others)

Things become pretty simple don't they?

Now every business is different... So my intention in this Book is to give you a broad perspective by which to analyse your business. I will give you a multitude of strategies to increase the **Golden Ratios** in your business.

Simply choose the appropriate strategies that serve you and tweak where necessary. In the words of Bruce Lee - Anything you feel is relevant to you, "accept it and use it, add what is uniquely your own and discard the rest."

Just don't forget, No matter what business you are in. No matter what you sell, who you sell it to? Or where you want to sell it? As you have seen the Average Lifetime Profit Calculation applies to you. All the strategies may not apply but the System behind them certainly does.

Remember the System is more valuable than the strategies.
That's deep.

Welcome to "The Systems For Business Philosophy."

Let's conjure up some winds.

Key Takeaways From PART 1 - INTRODUCTIONS;
(You Fill In Here)

1. ....

....

....

....

2. ....

....

....

....

3. ....

....

....

....

4. ....

....

....

....

5. ....

....

....

Your Business History

List an experience from your past that is explained by the philosophies in this introduction.

....

....

....

....

....

....

....

....

....

....

....

....

....

....

PART 2:
DISCOVER THE FIRST '22 STRATEGIES YOU MUST APPLY TO DOUBLE TO NET PROFITS IN YOUR BUSINESS WITHIN THE NEXT 24 MONTHS OR LESS'

In 756 BC, the Chinese General Zhang Xun, and his army were under attack. The enemy was larger, stronger and possessed a wealth of resources. Zhang and his army were holed up in the castle, unable to even retaliate because they had run out of arrows.

One night Zhang came up with a great plan. He ordered his men to gather all the straw from around the grounds. They then wrapped up the straw in black sheet to resemble soldiers.

Zhang waited until dawn, and slowly lowered 1000 straw men over the walls, staging an attack. The enemy immediately responded by firing thousands of arrows into the men. Zhang had his army then pull the straw men back over the walls. Zhang in one swoop had routed the enemy's resources whilst replacing his own.

The following night Zhang ordered his men to again, lower the straw soldiers over the walls, though this time the Enemy was too clever to respond.

Again the third night the General ordered men over the walls, again the enemy were too clever to respond. Though this time he used real soldiers, and once on the ground the army staged a surprise attack and defeated a larger and underprepared enemy.

By using the power of Strategy, Zhang was able to build resources, create opportunities and overcome what were perceived by everyone else to be insurmountable odds.

PROFIT MAXIMISER # 1 - LEAD GENERATION

A WORD OF WARNING BEFORE WE BEGIN: If you don't yet know what your Average Lifetime Value of a Client is, you should NOT be trying to get new leads... We are certain you will be wasting money, time, resources and precious allocations.

You can download your Average Lifetime Value of a Client Template below; I have also included a quick 5-minute video there for you to work out your Lifetime Value Calculation.

www.thesystemsforbusiness.com/lifetimevalue

To expand on a previous statement 'One of the biggest and easiest mistakes to make in life and business... Is to look externally before you have reaped your internal goldmine.'

Lead Generation was primarily what I was referring to there. If you have a basic understanding of Direct Response Marketing you should be able to create new leads for your business.

However using conventional methods such as paid advertising... This is not always the best way to grow a business...

As Dan Kennedy explains... 'The most expensive thing you can do in business is get a new client.' Most of the time, it's better, faster, easier and cheaper to mine your existing list of resources before you look to get more leads. This book is a deep exploration of this theory.

Within any business there cash to be had within the next 7 days, just sitting there waiting to be strategically mined. The resources you need to achieve your goals probably already exist. So start thinking strategically before you look to spend more to make more.

If you forget this great business truth, you will end up with a poor and reactive strategy, a poor relationship with wealth generation and an under optimised, underutilised and underperforming business asset.

As a result of this, and my intention for you to understand how the whole system works before you look to scale it... I have broken up the lead generation and sales strategies in this book into two parts, philosophy and action. I will present the philosophy in the chapters to follow and I will tie everything together in the last section of the book with 3 more lead generation and sales strategies.

My first mentor Lachlan Cameron Came out with one of the wisest statements I've heard when I recorded a Podcast with him...

'People don't break... Systems do!'

In this statement Lachlan gave me the inspiration for the Business behind this book, 'Systems For Business,' because I saw..."Businesses Don't Break... Systems Do"

So let's explore these systems together...

But before we begin... Could you expand from linear to 'Geometric Thinking' in your business? Because there are 3 major sequences of any sale.'

1. Before the Sale
2. During the Sale
3. After the Sale

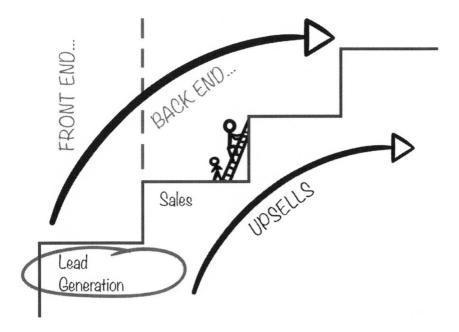

For lead generation we are dealing with what happens before the sale. And more specifically positioning prospective clients to put their hand up and ask to do business with you.

The goal of great lead generation is to get people **pre-interested, pre-disposed and pre-qualified** to do business with you on your terms **whilst ensuring the demand is always greater than supply in your business.**

Think of it this way... If you don't have a system for generating a Lead you know will cost you $25, and then based off your Sales Conversion Rates on those leads of 20% you are certain this will mean an average of $500 upfront that week to your business and then $3000 via ways of residual income in the coming months and years...

You may find yourself in the 95% of businesses who fail...

Lead Generation Marketing done correctly should never be a cost, but a viable investment, which provides you with a measureable return the stock market, could never consistently manage.

In the example above... You spend $125 to make a $500 cash sale, and due to your average lifetime repeat purchases, referrals and upsells you have accrued $3000 in income over the client lifecycle...

That's a 2800% Return on Investment...

Most business owner's are too stuck in linear thinking and as Mark Twain once said, 'When you find yourself on the side of the majority it's time to pause and reflect.'

BUSINESS BREAKTHROUGH QUESTION; What do you need before you can make a Sale? Can you position your marketing process around these requirements?

Let's get into the strategies...

STRATEGY 1 – Build Your Business Around Your Dream Client

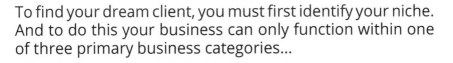

To find your dream client, you must first identify your niche. And to do this your business can only function within one of three primary business categories...

Health, wealth, or relationships...

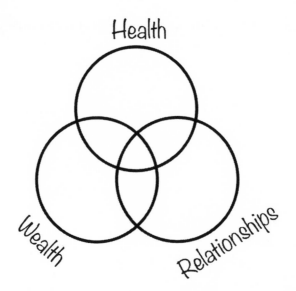

We will also be taking it two levels deeper. It's not enough to say I run a health business, this means nothing to nobody.

Within the Three Primary Business Categories you will find Markets of which there are thousands.

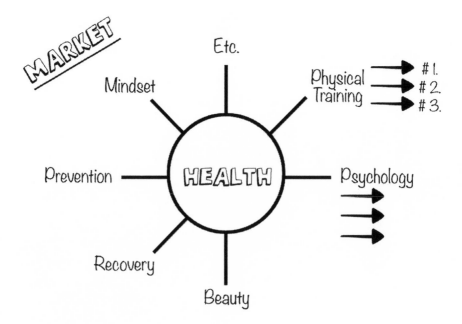

For example in the Health Category, you have mindset, physical training, psychology, recovery, prevention and beauty to name a few. But it's not just enough to say I'm a recovery business? I'm a mindset business? I'm a physical training business?

What does this really mean? Nothing to nobody... However if you take it one level deeper you will find the Niche... This is where you want to position your business. Right in an area that is thinly defined and preferably deep.

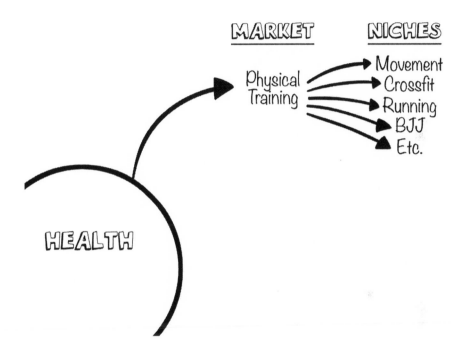

If I was to tell you I was a Cross-fit Coach, a Yoga Instructor or a Brazilian Jiu Jitsu Instructor... Now we're starting to get some clarity.

But we can even take it one level deeper than this... Who are you a Yoga Instructor for?

What sort of person do you serve within your Niche Market?

Exercise - Fill in your niche profile below...

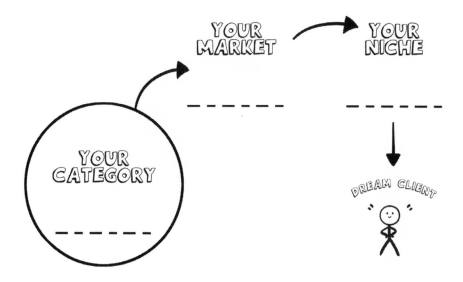

HOW TO ATTRACT YOUR DREAM CLIENT

What are the primary drivers causing your prospects and clients to take action?

Remember you have to *'enter the conversation they are having in their mind.'*

You have to enter in through their emotional filters... **What are their fears, frustrations, wants, needs and desires?** You can't simply produce rational messages because these messages will forever keep your business limited at steady, stagnant, and expected straight lines.

This is the starting point of your business. You need to know who its for because all of your communication from here on out will be directed solely and completely to this person only.

One of the biggest issues I see in business is when people approach me and say...

"Ben, my product is for everyone."

And I say, "Well, that's great, but I'd like you to imagine the following scenarios..."

I am an Australian male I live in Los Angeles. And next door to me there is another Australian male. We are both single. We are both the same age. Statistically speaking we are extremely similar. We are both Expats. We both make the same amount of money. The layout of our apartment is identical.

However when you walk into our apartments, you immediately realise the depth of difference. The art on the walls, the book in the shelves, even down to the smell of food and the colour of the couch...

Our demographic profile is the same but our psychographic profile is completely different.

It's the psychographics that determine much of our buying behaviour and they include things like our values, attitudes and beliefs.

Another example...

John is a 35-year-old man, who is single. He's working full-time in his job and he hates his job. He goes out a lot on the weekends, partying with some younger friends.

Mark on the other hand, is a 35-year-old man who is married and he has two children. He also hates his job. But he is extremely worried about how he's going to send his children to private schools.

Looking at Mark and John, they are in the same career, which they both hate and they are the same age.

Demographically they are quite similar. However, the emotional drivers causing them to action their buying behaviours are completely different.

If you were to put out a marketing message saying, "Attention: 35-year-olds who don't like their job" you may see a little bit of a result. But, if you approach this through the filter of speaking one-to-one, directly to Mark only, what you'll see is 100% to 1,000% to 10,000% greater response.

But still... I hear it almost everyday.

"This product/service is for everyone"

The problem with this statement is; your marketing must speak directly and only to prospects who are **pre-qualified, pre-interested and pre-disposed** to do business with you.

From there you can encourage them to seek YOUR solution to THEIR problem.

They don't perceive their problems through your filters.

They perceive it through their own.

Business Breakthrough Question – What business are you really in?

The more you target your marketing towards your thinly defined dream client... the cheaper, more effective and more efficient your marketing process will become.

There's a great old saying in marketing that *"we do not buy for rational reasons; we buy for emotional reasons and then we justify it rationally."*

95% of businesses fail because they run the 'rational' race...

I'm in the business of generating exponential curves for your business. And a proper understanding of who your Dream Client is... Can provide this for you.

To define your Dream Client we look to segments.

Each segment may define someone's reason to buy, or it may not, however it's best to have an idea of where your business touches each of these specific segments, as later on you will want to produce an advertising campaign, touching one or many of these elements.

BUSINESS BREAKTHROUGH QUESTION - WHO IS YOUR DREAM CLIENT?

A huge problem in the area of Marketing is that people are consistently looking at their current results and forecast the same for the future.

There is a reason I asked; **Who Is Your Dream Client?**

Because under the hood of this direct response marketing system you get to choose who you work with. How cool is that! Don't limit yourself before you begin. Why perceive limitations, lack of results or lack of harmony as a starting point?

BUINESS BREAKTHROUGH QUESTION – Who is Your 'Best Buyer?'

An excellent way to get started with your Dream Client is to model your existing favourite Client. Model their best aspects and as Bruce Lee said, 'Accept what is useful to you, add what is uniquely your own, and discard the rest"

Don't like their voice... Throw it out. Create the version of the Client you would love to serve on a daily basis. Who would you like to spend your time with?

Have a think right now about what are the key emotional drivers keeping your Dream Client up at night? This is where you must deliver your message into the heart and soul of your prospects.

Business Breakthrough Question - What are the 'Hair on Fire' problems your ideal client is facing? Could you build a business around serving these fears, frustrations, wants, needs and desires?

DREAM CLIENT SEGMENTS

1. DEMOGRAPHICS - are the statistically quantifiable data sets that define your prospects; Things like sex, age, height and Income. Demographics will inform some buying behaviour. But usually someone won't buy something just because they are a 35 year old. They may, but you need to think in more depth here.

2. PSYCHOGRAPHICS - are the study and classification of people according to their attitudes, aspirations, values, beliefs and other psychological criteria.

What Are Your Dream Clients VALUES; BONUS (What do They Secretly, Ardently Desire?)

Exercise - Fill in your dream client segments below...

BEHAVIOURS

GEOGRAPHY

UTILITY

DREAM CLIENT

PSYCHOGRAPHICS

DEMOGRAPHICS

STRATEGY 2 – Discover How to Use Education Based Marketing and Selling to Close Up to 500% More Sales

There are two distinct ways to use 'education based marketing and selling'. The first is using market data and the second is through the 'Four Slices of Interest.' If we consider the use of stories to be the Trojan horse gaining us safe passage into the castle, the use of market data could be best thought of as the German Blitzkrieg.

"Market data is way more motivational than product data"
- Chet Holmes

Let me illustrate...

I'd like you to imagine that you are in a big hall right now, and there are a thousand people in the room and we're at a women's health conference.

As I get up on the stage. The room goes silent. Everyone is looking up at me. And I say, "Hey, guys! My name is Ben Slater. I'm a nutritionist. Today, I want to talk to you about a nutrition program that will show you how to lose weight, whilst maintaining your energy, and still eating the foods you want" and I proceed to talk about my product or service.

Pretty good headline wasn't it? I probably could have widened the polarity by doing one focussed on me. But keep it in mind because that's what we're going to test against now.

In Presentation B, I get up onto the stage. Again, crowd is silent. Everyone is looking up at me.

"The number 2 killer in the country is Cancer....

Does anyone here know what the prevalence of breast cancer was in 1940?

It was 1 in 20...

In the 1990's, this had risen to 1 in 8 is going to get breast cancer...

It's the number 1 killer of women between the ages of 40 and 55.

Every other person is going to get cancer at some stage of her life. So, I'd like you to look to the person next to you – look them in the eyes and decide which one of you is going to get cancer – because that's the reality of the situation we're facing today.

So... My name is Ben Slater, I'm a nutritionist and I have done a huge study on the background of this cancer, why it exists and how we can get rid of it. Are you guys are interested in hearing a little bit more about that today?"

Yes, that's a pretty extreme example. However, for the purposes of what I'm trying to show you right now, those are real statistics. And I just showed up in a tank. Which one do you think would be more effective? Which sales presentation do you think would close more orders and therefore allow me as the Nutritionist to help more people?

Now, what I'm doing there is implementing a process called education-based selling. I'm using statistics and real market data to increase shock, awe and emotion and drive home my key points. This makes things exponentially more powerful in the marketing and sales environment.

The second way to use 'Education Based Marketing and Selling' is through an understanding of a philosophy I call the "Four Slices of Interest."

Let me illustrate...

In any room of people, and let's take it back to the same room. I could ask the room, "How many people are in the market to buy a car right now?" and what you'll typically see is about three percent of hands in the room will rise. I could ask, "How many people are in the market to buy a house right now?" and what you'll typically see, If the sample size is big enough approximately one to three percent of the room would raise their hands. If I was to ask, "how many people in the room are interested in purchasing a nutrition product right now?" Typically, again, three percent, would raise their hands.

This is where the majority of businesses and your competition are focusing their marketing and sales strategy.

"Hey! You want to buy something. I've got the product. Awesome! I can do that. Let's do that!" "You want to buy a bikini? Great! I sell bikinis! Fantastic!"

If I was to ask a question at the event, "How many people are interested in buying a house but they don't have enough information to make the right buying decision right now?" What you'll typically see is about 30 percent of hands in the room would rise – 30 percent versus three percent. Ten times more hands in that room just need a little bit more information. They need education.

The next question to ask: "How many people in this room, within the next few years, are going to be making a buying decision in purchasing a house and, in that period, you would love to be educated on how to make the buying decision, therefore when the time comes, you're going to be ready and prepared to make it?" Another 30 percent of hands in the room would rise again. We've gone from three percent to 60 percent, which makes up 63 percent of the room.

And what about the other 37 percent? We can round it out by asking, "Who knows they're not in the market to buy a house in the next 5 years and they are not going to be interested in education?" Roughly 37 percent of hands will rise in that room.

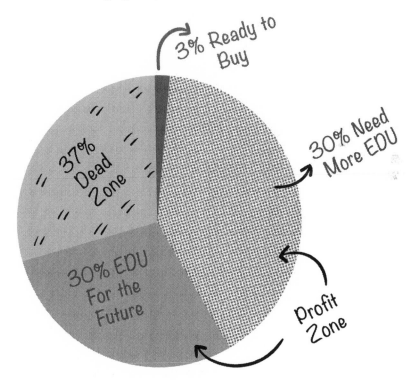

Next time you're in a room of 100 people test it out.

By adopting an 'Education-Based Marketing and Selling' approach, you can access a market that is roughly twenty times larger than the one that your competitors are focusing on. And when you mix this with Telling stories, Strategy 2 & 3 - Developing Bigger, Better (Educational) Baits and Strategy 25 Turning Prospects Into Paying Clients. You have everything you need to build a business that is rapidly growing business.

You should find some market data to Blitzkrieg your market.

For example: "Did you know that 95 percent of small businesses fail within ten years? And did you know that 50 percent of businesses fail over 18 months? And did you know that the average wage in Australia has risen to over $79,000 – Australian dollars per year – one of the highest in the world?"

These statistics are all examples of things you can use to drive home your point. Do you think it's polarizing for the business owner who realizes they're making just above or less money than the average person in Australia? Do you think they're going to be more likely to take action on some of the strategies in this book once they realize?

BUSINESS BREAKTHROUGH QUESTION – Which of the '4 Slices of Interest' are you speaking to in your marketing right now?

ACTION ITEM – Employ someone on 'Upwork' to find 20 pieces of market data you can use to Blitzkrieg your market.

STRATEGY 3 – Discover How to Use Bigger Better Baits to Attract Higher Quality Clients

I would like you to imagine you are at a fishing pond of your choice, and in this fishing pond, as you stand on the edge looking in, your ambitions are highly charged. Today you are looking to reel in some prize fish.

Now, if that's the case, what sort of bait have you brought with you? Did you bring some little shrimp? Or did you bring something large, and more likely to appeal to your intended captor?

If you were going out on the ocean to catch marlin, what sort of fish would you bring then? Would you bring that same shrimp?

This is exactly what we're talking about, in regards to your Lead Generation.

One of the biggest mistakes I see business owners consistently making is that they don't spend enough time, effort or energy to develop the right assets for their business. Therefore, they stay stuck and forever at the whim of economic cycles.

If you want to attract the right clients into your business, if you want to prove that you are serious , then you need to realize that marketing – direct response marketing – is the most important use of your time.

Could you stop trying to sell your products and services and develop a marketing asset that positions you an the preeminent expert in your field, whilst getting your prospective clients pre-qualified, pre-interested and pre-disposed to do business with you?

Direct response marketing done correctly is literally salesmanship via print. These minutes spent appropriately will continue to work for you for the weeks, months and years to come. It's a highly leveraged activity.

Think of it this way. I have produced this message once and it's in the hands of thousands of people. Yeah it took me a few weeks in Patagonia, Argentina, to write it, but this was some of the most leveraged, impactful, and income-generating work I've ever produced.

You too, can produce a message once that goes out to hundreds, thousands, maybe even hundreds of thousands of people at the same time. And if you're telling me you don't have the time to develop that resource, then you may never reach scale. You may never reach the amount of people you could. And frankly, you are completely self-sabotaging how good you are at delivery.

I'd like you to imagine that you're in a food court right now. You have all of your ideal clients and all of your ideal prospects in the food court. They're all eating. They're all having a good time. They're having conversations. They're enjoying themselves.

All of a sudden, you grab a chair and you stand up and scream out your offer.

I often quiz business owners on the Food Court Test and 90% of the time people either have no idea what to say or they try and sell...

"I'm Ben and you should pay me now to take my consulting"

How many people approached you to take action? How many people come up to you and said, "Oh, Ben, that's amazing! Here, sign me up right now! Here's my credit card details, here's my email, phone number and home address in-case you want to come over for tea..."

C'mon... It went horribly... Because not everyone in this this slice wants to be told what to do. Trust still needs to be built first.

The food court test is exactly what you are doing in your business right now. There is no difference between the modern world of social media, print, radio or online marketing as there is from the modern world of the food court.

Now, if you cannot imagine your offer would be successful in that food court, why the hell would your offer be successful online? They're even more distracted online.

These are the sorts of thinking principles you need to apply to your business. If your offer isn't getting people scrambling up out of their seats, tearing each other apart, then you know you are off the mark.

So how can you rig your success a little more and orchestrate this savagery? By using a concept from the excellent book, 'The Irresistible Offer' by Mark Joyner. Mark says the 'Irresistible Offer' must have three specific components.

The first component is a **High Return on Investment Offer.**

This means, for whatever this person is going to give you, they're going to have to rationalize something to themselves. (This concept is so important I've dedicated the whole of Strategy 14 to it.)

The inner most dominant thought of the prospect at the time of engagement is; "What's in it for me? Am I getting a greater return on what I'm giving here?"

Are you asking for the order? Or are you asking for the email address? Or possibly the phone number, and physical address.

What are you giving in return for this investment and how are you presenting your offer? If your prospects don't clearly see they're getting a direct and measurable return on investment – on their time, their money, their relationships, or their freedom, you're not going to get their time or money.

Now, the second element is a **Touchstone.**

A touchstone is a little slogan, subtitle or a heading that succinctly describes exactly what benefit they're going to get. They could even remember it and tell it to others.

Now, that is a touchstone.

A fantastic example of this is Domino's Pizza. Domino's built a multibillion-dollar-business off the back of this single touchstone.

"Fresh, piping hot pizza, delivered to your door in 30 minutes or less – or it's free!"

The third aspect of the irresistible offer is **Believability.**

In the world of business today – and because we are so bombarded by messages – it's said that we see up to 5,000 advertising messages per day. To maintain sanity, and protect the castle we reject so much of the marketing we see.

What this means... If you're presenting offers that aren't really believable from the perspective of the prospect with their base of knowledge and not yours, then you're putting yourself at serious disadvantage when it comes to marketing today.

And to remove the curtain for you... I will show you exactly how I've done this in the book that you're holding in your hands.

My high return on investment offer; you have given me your email address, your physical address, your phone number and your credit card details for a small purchase.

And you are committing 3-4 hours of time to read this book.

By using my touchstone, I was able to communicate why you should do all these things...

"The Business Owner's Guide to Profit; Discover 25 Strategies You Must Apply to Double the NET Profits in YOUR Business Without Trading More Time, More Money, Ruining Any More Relationships or Bastardising Your Purpose"

As a business owner reading this, were you thinking, "I could give my email address, my phone number, pay a small fee for the book and spend a few hours of my time reading this book..."

Do you think all those things that I've just mentioned are a pretty good trade-off to double the net profits in your business in the next 24 months or less?

Also, the last one, you'll notice I'm not promising you can move to Fiji in the next 7 weeks, make seven figures while you sit on a beach in your underwear and drink 7 mojitos. I'm promising if you apply these strategies, if you understand and follow the path, and if you understand, follow the path and simply implement the relevant strategies over the next 24 months. You'll be able to double your NET profits. There's a high degree of believability in the offer that I'm giving you right now.

BUSINESS BREAKTHROUGH QUESTION - What Are You Yelling Out in the Food Court?

ACTION ITEM – Sit down and plan out your offer.... What is your 'High Return on Investment' Offer? What is your 'Touchstone?' How 'Believable' is your offer? Get to work on structuring this offer. Make it bigger, make it better, and make it irresistible bait.

ACTION ITEM – If you want to succeed in business you must become a serious student of marketing. Marketing becomes a lot easier when you model what other smart marketers are doing. Create swipe files to save effective advertisements you see. Create a process document or cheat sheet in your business that collects various tools such as 'The Irresistible Offer.' Use this form as a filter to refine your offers.

STRATEGY 4 – NEVER WANT TO PAY FOR MARKETING AGAIN? FORM, MINE AND MANUFACTURE STRATEGIC PARTNERSHIPS

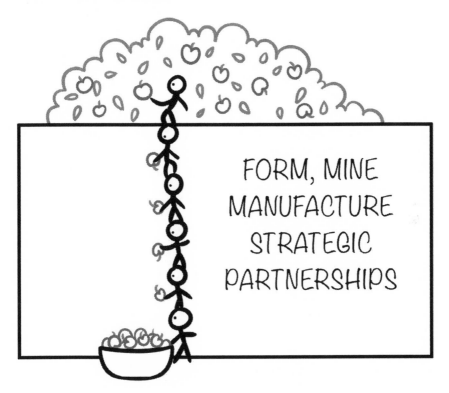

In August of 2016 – I set out to start a personal development business. I set the objective when I started this business. I wanted to start it with zero capital. I didn't have to do this at the time but it was something I wanted to challenge myself to do and (maybe self righteously) prove a few of my concepts and show my clients it was possible to do the same.

I set out to follow the most effective way I know of to build a business with no capital. I set out to build strategic partnerships.

I asked myself some important Questions, *"Who has access to my ideal clients?"*

And, *"What happens before and after my clients do business with me?"*

The path to personal development and business has a common root or starting point in Health and Fitness. Before people turn their attention into the mind, they have commonly focused on the body. The best way to master your psychology is to master your physiology so it's only a natural progression for people interested in health and fitness to focus on personal development.

Before I became a business consultant, I had run an online health and fitness business. I had come from this industry, so I reached out to a bunch of contacts I had. And there's one specific partnership that comes to mind.

As a bit of context, I was running a $600 personal development event. It was a one-day event where I share my knowledge on the seven key areas of life. I asked myself a question and it's a question that every single business owner should ask...

Business Breakthrough Question - *"How much can I afford to pay to make a sale?"*

This is the most important piece of knowledge to have in marketing because most people just pay this to Facebook, or to Google, or even blow it up against the wall by running 'brand building' and non direct marketing campaigns.

A big mistake business owners make is they ask... *"How much can I afford to pay for a lead,"* but the lead is secondary. It's the sale you should be focussed on. At times more expensive leads will convert higher into sales, and vice versa. There is no rational reason to track lead cost over the cost of sale. It's an important metric yes. But there are more important considerations to be made.

"What if you could pay someone who had a direct and measurable line to the people that could pay you?"

Here's what's completely mind-blowing.

Because you are borrowing the trust of someone else, you can boost your business and boost your own level of trust beyond what you could normally acquire. As trust is the most important feature in the mind of your prospects, you can achieve results you wouldn't be able to find elsewhere.

So how much could I afford to pay to make a sale? It was $300.

And at this stage you might be thinking, *"Ben, under no circumstances do I want to give away 50% of my revenue per unit to make a sale"*

Hold tight because we'll get more into back-end systems and on selling from events in the strategies to come. But, as a quick bit of context, I was aware that, at the event, I would close a minimum of 10 percent of the room into a product that was ten times more expensive than the original $600. So, armed with my some basic mathematics, I knew I could even go negative at the event – Even lose money at the event – and still make good money on the back-end.

I have some good friends who run a large podcast. I called them up and told them I was running the event. Instead of sponsoring the podcast via an ad, they interviewed me and I did a soft pitch at the end. What I arranged with them was; Any sales made off the back of this arrangement, I would pay $300 per sale I made – Which was more than I would have paid them if I had advertised on the platform.

This is the golden key to strategic partnerships. You always pay more. Find a way to make both parties benefit and only pay for sales, not leads.

Therefore you build a more powerful relationship because this is return on investment thinking. You must remember these are strategic partners who have access to your niche! If you reward them for that, you're going to be rewarded. This is very powerful and leveraged thinking.

So... That was the deal – $300 to make a sale.

Now, I went on the podcast, I had some inquiries off the back of it, and I believe – through this specific strategic partnership arrangement - I made six sales. That's $3600 in sales and, of that, half went to the affiliate, half stayed with me.

But the real gold in this is the upsells at the back of the event...

I sold 50 tickets to the Seed of Life event. I made $22,500 – that's aggregate of the cash that I made minus the affiliate fees on the front end. And In the week after the event, I made $69,000 in sales off the back end.

So by doing a rough Lifetime Revenue Calculation on these tickets they move from an average of $450 per person seated to $1830 per person.

You can see, I know my numbers and because I know the Lifetime Value of a Client, I was able to easily give away the $300. It makes perfect sense. It's an excellent offer for the affiliate and it's an excellent offer for me.

So for where you're at right now, the great question to ask is; who has access to your ideal prospects? Think outside of Facebook. Think outside of the normal lines. The best avenues are untapped by the majority of the market.

I heard a fantastic story the other day of a Gym in Sydney... This gym realized - all of their ideal prospects were hanging out in a café nearby, eating health food and socializing.

So, they approached the cafés owner, "Hey, can we come in and buy everyone's coffees? And in exchange for buying everyone's coffees, can we grab some emails and phone numbers? And follow up with them"

GENIUS...

From the perspective of the business owner, he's going to get coffees bought for all his clients, which is awesome for them; this creates a buzz and gets people in the door to try the coffee. Some of these people will become repeat clients – and for the Gym Owner it cost them $3.00 to buy the coffees – The gym, is getting all these contact details of their ideal prospects for $3.00.

Now, when they called these people up. Without me knowing their specific numbers a typical gym – will have a lifetime value of a client anywhere between $5000 to $15,000 to get someone signed up and in the door.

Now if you're crunching the numbers, which I know you are... What percentage of people do they have to close to get a return on investment?

Absolutely ridiculous amounts of leverage achieved here.

Lets imagine they bought 1000 coffees for $3000. They acquire 1000 leads for $3000. They close just one in the first twenty and they have made a Return on Investment. Who knows how far they take this. They may end up like my old client's, Shaun and Matt from CrossFit Agilis in Sydney, famously said in a casestudy video... "We need a bigger gym"

If you don't know it yet, you're leaving hundreds of thousands of dollars on the table.

BUSINESS BREAKTHROUGH QUESTION - Who are your strategic partners?

Write a list. Who are the people you can build relationships with? They don't have to exist right now. You form, you mine and then manufacture – these are the three elements of strategic partnership building.

Be intentional. You should have a list of people who you're working through, who you're actively building relationships with, and you're offering irresistible High Return On Investment offers to help build your business while you help them build theirs.

If you can combine the irresistible offer with strategic partnerships, you will never have to pay for marketing again. You could only pay for sales, which is a very financially empowering study.

BUSINESS BREAKTHROUGH QUESTION - "How much can I afford to pay to make the sale?"

ACTION ITEM – "Who has access to your ideal Clients?" Write a list of 25-50 potential strategic partners you could combine forces with. Have a look at your front end and back end numbers... Once you have read the book. Develop your strategy for pitching the partners. The next few chapters should help with this. It's important to remember in strategic partnerships you must ensure the partner has little to no work to do in the relationship.

ACTION ITEM – When you build your bigger, better client funnel; ruthlessly track your metrics so that you know exactly what you can afford to pay for a sale and for a lead. You will want to generate at least 100 leads to test your system before jumping to conclusions about your return on investment. These stats will inform your offer to your strategic partners.

STRATEGY 5 – 80/20 Sales and Marketing

In all of the businesses I've consulted with, I have noticed a pattern. The majority of these businesses have the desired outcome flipped in reverse. They spend 80 percent of their time on delivery and 'other' things I put into delivery box because they're not directly income producing – such as branding.

Note; Under this new system, you're currently being exposed to, anything that is not direct response marketing or sales is an expense to your business.

The majority of businesses are spending 20 percent of their time on marketing and sales, and 80 percent of their time on delivery. What would happen in your business if you flipped it? What would happen in your business if you spent 80 percent of your time on sales and marketing, and 20 percent of your time on delivery?

As you move beyond the million dollar mark you could look to spend more time on delivery from there once you have dialled in your marketing and sales processes.

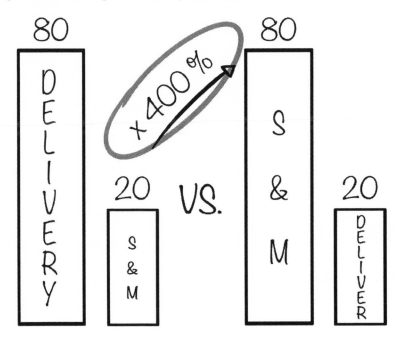

Now the effect of this is two-pronged because firstly it forces you to spend 400 percent more time on marketing and sales which, mathematically speaking, without assuming you will get better at both, you would make 400 percent more money. Secondly, because you're condensing the amount of time you have to deliver, you have to find a way to leverage your delivery. You can't lose anything you need. You can't deliver less of a product or a service. You are then forced to apply leverage and stop focussing on things that don't matter.

I hope you are beginning to see... "I can get more without doing more!" Which is really the premise, goal and intention of this book. It's to awaken you to this new system. To awaken you to how you are currently using your resources and to lovingly polarize you a little bit on some areas you could be optimizing and improving. If you implement your learning's I'm certain you are going to achieve the touchstone of this book which is to double the net profits in your business, which makes me very happy.

So at, 'The Seed of Life' and 'Systems for Business...' We literally break up the calendar into 80 percent Marketing and Sales, and 20 percent delivery. I put our delivery at the end of the day and our marketing at the start of the day. This optimizes the business to make sure everyone is focused on the right objectives every day.

How this impacts the lead generation is because you are becoming more empowered in your business. You are focussing on directly income producing items, and it's likely you will be spending at least 400% more time, effort and energy to build your business. The ripple effect is huge. Something else to consider here, is that your time becomes more valuable per hour because you are optimising it for income generation.

ACTION ITEM - Restructure your business from next week for '80/20 Sales and Marketing.' Brace yourself because this one strategy could literally double the NET profits in your business and cause a few waves in the process.

How much of your time is now allocated towards Marketing and Sales?

_____

How much of your time is now allocated towards Delivery?

_____

What changes will you make as a result?

_____

Key Takeaways From The Lead Generation Section;
(You Fill In Here)

1. ....

....

....

....

2. ....

....

....

....

3. ....

....

....

....

4. ....

....

....

....

5. ....

....

....

Your Business History

List an experience from your past that is explained by the strategies in the Lead Generation Section.

List 5 Ideas For New Strategies to Increase Your Lead Generation;
(You Fill In Here)

1. ....
....
....
....

2. ....
....
....
....

3. ....
....
....
....

4. ....
....
....
....

5. ....
....

PROFIT MAXIMISER # 2; SALES CONVERSIONS %

Here's the best definition of sales I have ever heard...

"Sales is getting people intellectually involved in a future result that is good for them and then getting them to commit emotionally to get that result"

–Dan Sullivan

STRATEGY 6 – Discover the Single Most Important Aspect of Sales

I'd like you to imagine you are 25 years old and you are in a room with 99 other 25 year olds. As you look around you notice they've all got a certain sparkle in their eye, they're all just about to set out into their careers and their continued journeys. At the front of the room, I say unto you, "Can I see a show of hands, who's going to be successful in their lives?"

You wonder if it's a trick question. You look around as one hundred hands rise in that room.

Now what's the reality?

By age 65... 5 People will become financially independent and 1 "lucky" soul becomes what we could term "wealthy"?

I know everyone has different ideas about what success means. But, at the end of the day, financial empowerment is one of the seven major areas of life. And if you're lying to yourself about it's benefits. Or that ability to serve your values and your ability to serve others wouldn't drastically increase because of it.

C'mon you're an entrepreneur for god's sake. Accept the inarguable conclusion that striving for personal wealth is one of the noblest quests we can undertake in our own lives.

Every extra dollar you earn increases your ability to add more value into the world.

My major question to you is this;

"Why is it that there's such a diathesis between the things that we are saying we want and the things that happen?"

I believe this is due to a lack of education and therefore 95 percent of people focus on the money! They focus on the thing they want and it's the one thing that avoids them.

How fascinating. This is the nature of polarity. Just like night follows day, summer chases winter and hot confronts cold. Everything in the world is formed of two conflicting elements that build the whole. And in the Human Psyche, when you emotionally attach to one thing you unconsciously produce the other.

Contrary to what most people believe... Entrepreneurship is the most selfless exercise you can involve yourself in. Because to grow you have to consciously detach yourself from your needs, wants and desires... And only then do you advance them.

You cannot ignore the universal laws that govern nature because they also govern the Psyche. And as a result the most important area of study for any entrepreneur is personal development.

This is a consulting business, yes. But I also run a personal development business and I do this because the two are so inextricably linked. You cannot have one without the other and I've tried it. It doesn't work.

The greatest secret to my Success is Business is that it's 80% Mindset and 20% strategy. So in saying this, if you're loving this book so far, you would be at least 400% better off in your business by following me here too... www.theseedof.life

As Entrepreneurs we shouldn't be seeking money, which sounds strange to say, but it's why the most successful amongst us always seek growth, contribution and self worth. These are the elements that combine to supply willpower.

So how can you master sales? Firstly you need to master your mindset and learn how to control it. I have not once seen a problem in Business that doesn't stem from one of the 7 personal areas of life. What you perceive you're worth is where you'll forever keep yourself limited in business. The self image is forever the limit of belief. And where belief ends so does the business.

The best quality and quantity we can chase in life is not money it's self-worth.

It's why 95% of people never acquire the thing they chase so desperately. They have too much of an external frame of mind. They think it's outside of them, but in reality your success is inside of you.

My solution to this problem is to increase self-worth on a daily, weekly, monthly, yearly basis. Every single day, I'm doing it. The Seed of Life System involves improving the seven contrasting and conflicting elements in your life. And then scoring yourself on these areas everyday.

The 7 areas of life include physical health, social empowerment and family dynamics. This is what I term the 'Yin of Life.' And then we have 'The Yang of Life,' including personal finance, career development and intellect.

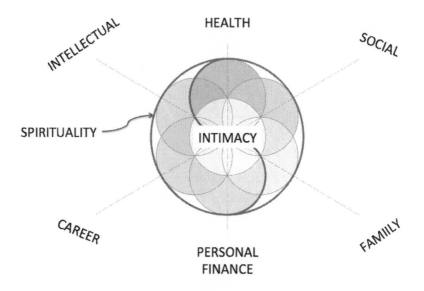

The last area is sexual intimacy, which is the area most commonly repressed within our lives. Also, once you combine all of those elements into the whole, you have true spirituality.

Albert Einstein once said, "The most beautiful thing we can experience is the mysterious. It is the source of all true art and science. He to whom the emotion is a stranger, who can no longer pause to wonder and stand wrapped in awe, is as good as dead —his eyes are closed. The insight into the mystery of life, coupled though it be with fear, has also given rise to religion. To know what is impenetrable to us really exists, manifesting itself as the highest wisdom and the most radiant beauty, which our dull faculties can comprehend only in their most primitive forms—this knowledge, this feeling is at the centre of true religiousness."

I follow the belief that true religiosity involves loving yourself enough to grow because it's what I believe we are all here to. Can you combine all 7 colours of your spectrum into the core and become a bright light.

Spirituality isn't about believing in some guy up there with a white beard, who has an imaginary power over you. It's about loving yourself enough to cherish your own life. To not try to change others but to only change yourself because when you do the whole world will rise.

I like to think of the 'Seed of Life' as the 7 octaves on the piano. When you only focus on only one area of life. You forever damn yourself to play 'Mary Had a Little Lamb.' But when you learn about your nature, when you discover, differentiate then integrate your personality, you have mastered the other 6 areas of your life.

And then... Who knows how well you could play?

As Pythagoras told us, *"there is music in the spacing of the spheres."*

When you improve your self image through the system I've developed at the Seed of Life, you will intrinsically start to command more value. If you don't have a system for improving all of those seven areas of life, I guarantee you, your business will self-sabotage to teach you to love the areas of yourself you have forgotten.

If you want to master sales, if you want to master business growth, if you want to make more money, then you must master those other areas. We have 7 bank accounts in life and these conflicting and contrasting elements all make up the whole. You cannot get past this. You cannot spend your life focusing purely on the yang side of life and ignore the yin. You can't ignore health, your family or social interactions, because the universe will create a situation that rocks you to the core and demolishes your business. Which, funnily enough, will be exactly what you need.

This system I've briefly shared with you is how I rebuilt myself from mental illness, and the most profound thing I've discovered in it all... It's a spectrum. The same system that moved me from schizophrenia to psychosis to depression to anxiety is the same system that moved me from mediocrity into a very elementary level of mastery in Personal and Business development.

If you want a system for Mastering Your Mindset beyond what I've explained to you here. You should check out 'The Seed of Life' – It's an idea whose time has come in the world and I'm really grateful to be able to share it with you, as it's my primary purpose in life.

Business Breakthrough Question – Where are you more empowered in your life right now? Yin or Yang? What are 3 action items you can take next month to bring things back into balance?

ACTION ITEM – Score yourself out of 7 in the key areas of life right now. Draw a spider plot to see where you really are in your life. Remember what you need is what you don't have. You're only as empowered as your lowest point.

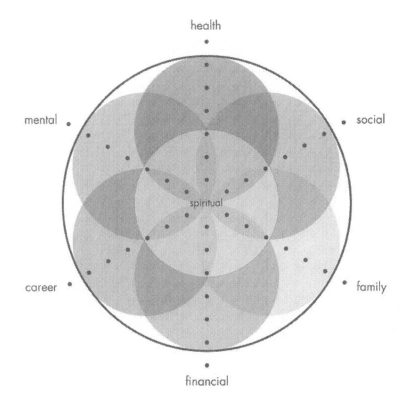

"Every now and then go away, have a little relaxation, for when you come back to your work your judgment will be surer. Go some distance away because then the work appears smaller and more of it can be taken in at a glance and a lack of harmony and proportion is more readily seen."

–Leonardo Da Vinci

ACTION ITEM - As a special offer to members of the Systems For Business Tribe; I will send you a free physical copy of my $49 daily accountability system when you cover P + H. Head www.theseedof.life/sfbtribe to claim yours today.

STRATEGY 7 - How to Create an Engagement Ladder to Sell 10% of Your Clients Into Products and Services 10x More Expensive

I got this idea from a guy called Russell Brunson, a brilliant marketer who runs a business called ClickFunnels.

The engagement ladder is a premise that looks a little bit like a staircase. I've included a picture of it just below. And In the staircase, there are multiple levels of your business.

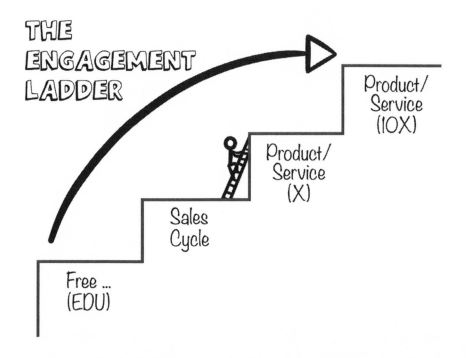

Step 1 is free. You're not trying to sell anyone here; you're trying to educate them on how to make a buying decision. Now that you understand Bigger Better Baits, this might come in the format of a book, webinar, a podcast series or something else of very high value that people are going to take action on in exchange for some contact details. We will delve more deeply into how to structure this towards the end of the book.

Next, after you've got their details, you've gained permission to follow up. In exchange for the 'free content', you collect permission assets. You will want to get as many emails, phone numbers, and physical addresses as possible and then plug them into your sales cycle.

Step 2 is your sales cycle. The best way for you to do this will depend on inner workings and objectives of your business, which we will also address towards the end of the book.

Step 3 is where you sell your first product and service. Every single business is going to be different so outside of an event or private consult I can't give you an answer on what this should be. However, what you want to do here is make sure that you are providing the most value possible, whilst being highly engaging and getting the most people through the door in your business.

During Step 3, the more trust you build with your clients the more back end sales and long-term relationships you build. Hold nothing back here. In my experience the best way to do this is an introductory seminar.

From there, Step 4 and beyond is the Back End. Where you make all of your profits by selling continuity based products and services... For example a month-by-month, mastermind marketng package worth $2,000 per month.

Let me use an example of my Personal Development Company and the engagement ladder I use there. I spoke earlier of the event that I ran – the Seed of Life Event. There were 50 people there. In terms of buying units in the room, a lot of them were my brother's clients who I didn't try and sell. So, there were about 35 buying units in the room.

Typically, what I base my theories of the engagement ladder off, when done properly, and when structured correctly, at least ten percent (and up to 50 percent in some circumstances) of people will buy something at an event, or during a course or program that is at least ten times more expensive.

As I mentioned earlier, I sold 50 tickets for an average of $600 income per person – then minus some of the affiliate fees off the top. So my average net income was $450. Looking at that, that's $22,500 for the event. At the end of the event, I sold a program that was $7,500. I had six people buy that, and I had three people join a consulting package.

On the back-end, I made approximately $70,000 in sales. Looking at those numbers, I made 8 sales and had about 35 buying units in the room. So 22.8% percent of the buying units in the room purchased something and all of these purchases were greater than ten times more expensive than the original ticket to the event.

Here's what it looks like.

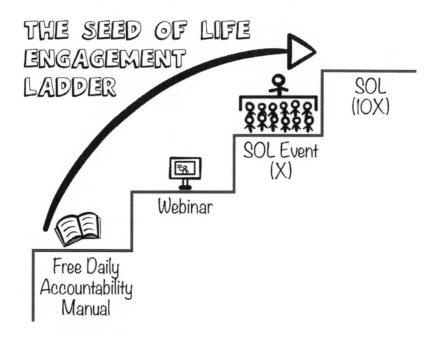

These strategies really work. They are open to all business when you do the work. When you study marketing and sales and you really understand what it is that people are looking for and you fill in those gaps.

It's easy to overcomplicate business at times...

Conversely I've noticed businesses that have an amazing front end, (and what I'm talking about when I say front-end is a website, an Instagram Page or a Facebook page – how it looks on the outside.) Often have no idea about the Back End.

The back-end is what's really happening on the inside. What's the strategy behind selling the product? What's happening after you've sold the product? Are there upsells? Are there down sells? Is this product purely lead generation? Is this your only one product?

You could think of the Front End as Profit Maximiser One – Lead Generation.

You could think of the Back End as Profit Maximisers two, three, four, five, six, seven and eight in this book.

Are you starting to realise why 95% of Businesses fail over 10 years?

Plugging a powerful and lead generating front end and a profit maximising back end is the way to do business. You should now make up to ten times more money in the back-end of your business than the front-end of your business.

Most businesses I see have no idea about back-end systems. Therefore, they keep themselves limited to less than ten percent of what they could achieve by adopting the simple strategy I've just mentioned here and I've just completely removed the curtain for you to see how I do it at events.

I've routinely closed 20 percent of the room into something ten times more expensive. You can do the same too. You can put in the work and see how it's done.

There's a great philosophy from Dan Kennedy and it's to always have the guts to ask the order every time. It's something that I always follow in business. If you are providing great value for people, then why not let that person go any further? This is the whole premise around the engagement ladder.

As they step up through the engagement ladder, they are

deepening their level of engagement with you. They're getting closer to you. If you build your business around an attractive character and you position yourself correctly – you can drive a lot of sales and enthusiasm around your business. These sorts of philosophies aren't that difficult. There is a before, during, and after to every sale.

BUSINESS BREAKTHROUGH QUESTION - "What happens before and what happens after your sale? Can you fill the gaps with extra products and services to serve your clients more?"

Your most qualified prospects are your clients. Your best leads in your business right now are the people that have bought from you before. They have a proven track record.

I have consulted with businesses that say, "No, we don't sell things that are more expensive. We don't do this" And unfortunately, Their fears around what money is, and how to ask for it, keeps their community really small.

I would recommend identifying those fears and dealing with them. I would ask that you actually step into it because, once you experience the sort of things I'm sharing with you right now, a new level of financial empowerment will be unleashed. You'll step into a different life. As a member of the 'Systems For Business Tribe,' that's what I see for you. To realise your fears of becoming a leader are less important than those people who are still going the through your prior struggles.

I'm not saying, "Go out there and try and make as much money as possible and not care about the people." What I'm trying to say to you is; go increase your self-worth enough to feel valuable, so that you can inspire other people to do the same.

Guess what happens when someone invests $5,000 in themselves? Do you think that's a huge shift in that person's life? Do you think that increases their self-worth more than anything they have ever done?

Every single time I've bought a program, a course or made one of these Investments in Self. I felt an initial: "Oh, I don't know if this is all right? Am I allowed to do this? Am I worthy of this?" And each time I follow through, I've felt this surge of appreciation for the fact that I'm investing in my own highest values and that I'm moving towards the person I want to become. It's available to each and every single one of you, but you have to start thinking strategically about who you are, what you've been through and what you have to offer.

Keep going. Never stop. There is no reason to stop making offers to your clients and prospects.

There's a great story Jay Abraham tells about a diabetes medication. He bought a pharmaceutical business. He then had a look through all of the records in the company. Because he had a great understanding of the Lifetime Value of a Client, what he realized was the business wasn't making enough sales on the front-end. However, once someone came into the business, they have purchased repeatedly every year, for something close to 16 times a year for 3.5 years on average. The lifetime value of a client, even though the medicine was quite cheap, was over $1,000.

Next, he contacted all of the stores that could sell the medication and said, "Hey! Here's this medication. Can you sell it for us? Instead of giving you the measly 20 percent like everyone else is giving to you, if you agree to put this in the right location, we'll give you 120 percent of the sales value. We'll give you more money than it costs if you give us the contact details of the person you sold it to."

He used front-end leverage to build the backend. Sales went through the roof. The lifetime value stayed the same. They sold that business after making an absolute killing – multi-millions of dollars in profits.

This is just one example of how you can think about front-end and back-end systems. Could you potentially go negative on the front-end to get a client, knowing full well that the back-end is going to be very profitable for you? Could you go negative at an event? Could you give 100 percent of the affiliate commissions to your strategic partners and have them do the sales for you? These are things that people do not even think about. Could you give 150 percent of the tickets from the event to people knowing full well you'll close ten percent of the room into something ten times more expensive?

At times you don't need more money, more time or more relationships to build a business. At first it seems crazy, but all you need is a strategic mind searching for leverage.

BUINESS BREAKTHROUGH QUESTION - Armed with your newfound understanding of Leverage could you allow someone else to do the legwork in building a business for you?

ACTION ITEM – Build your engagement ladder below;

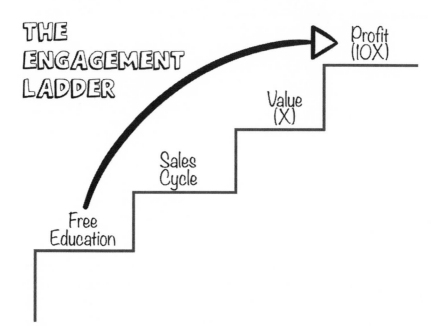

THE ENGAGEMENT LADDER

Free Education

Sales Cycle

Value (X)

Profit (10X)

STRATEGY 8 – Discover the $5000.00 Secret of Sales

In this chapter, I'm going to share with you my Secret Weapon of Sales...

I have a $5,000 investment to thank for this... A hard drive, bought from Jay Abraham, containing about 100 of his previous courses and programs on it. I bought the hard drive knowing the content contained within would have the power to change my business, and therefore yours too.

The biggest takeaway I got from the hard drive was the use of guarantees.

I realized that I wasn't guaranteeing anything in the selling environment, because I thought, "Well, why should I guarantee it? What if they don't take action? What if they have a mindset meltdown and don't do the work?"

I came up with all these reasons why I shouldn't make guarantees.

But then I came to a realization. It finally dawned on me that there are two people in the buying environment; and one of them is going to take on more risk than the other. If you assume the position of risk, you're going to make a lot more sales in your business.

Surprisingly, guarantees operate in the exact opposite frame than you'd think, because they take the responsibility off you, and put it on the client.

It has the opposite effect of what I originally thought it would have. I thought it would increase refunds. But they have gone down!

What I say is: "Try it and see what happens!" because I can guarantee your refunds will go down. There is something unconscious that occurs when you offer a guarantee towards someone.

I believe it goes something like this…

By offering the guarantee, you are standing behind what you do – 100 percent. You are planting your two feet on the ground. You are looking that person in the eyes and saying, "You can trust me because I have the system to help you."

Now, in the coaching and consulting space that I am in, the only way my products and services fail, is when the person has a mindset meltdown and decides not to do the things I'm asking. This is typically what you see in a coaching environment. As you can tell it would be pretty hard to not get a Return on Investment using these systems and strategies. Business owners are usually great at delivery but, at times, there are other factors that come in – relationships, health, family factors, financial factors, factors with purpose and direction, there's mental factors and even spiritual; these all play a role.

Now, when I guarantee my products and services, I am still protecting myself where I can because I get them to sign a contract and stipulate my terms in the contract. If the person is involved in "acts of God" as they're termed in the contract, am I liable to refund them?

Am I eligible if the person agrees, they are going to do something and they don't do it? Nope, that's not on me. I'm not here to enforce people's limitations, and lack of action. I'm not here to perpetuate people's nightmare. I'm here to exponentially grow your business using leverage so you don't have to trade away your time, money, relationships and freedom to get there.

What I suggest is; you create your unique version of the guarantee that works for you and the client, but also protects you from any ridiculous circumstances.

As a result of the impact this has had on my results, all the products and services that I offer in my business are guaranteed.

Here's one of them:

I run a $5000 AUD event. My guarantee is that I will work with one on one to increase the profits in your business. In this program, we build your Direct Response Marketing Systems, we build your Sales Systems, we have a look at your Lifetime Value Systems, and most importantly, I give you my Mindset Mastery System. We completely, and individually, optimize your business in a group setting, so you can leverage off the learning's from each other's businesses.

Now I know I am one of the only consultants in the industry that offers this type of guarantee and as you can see I am standing behind my products and services very strongly by doing so. I'm doing this because I am 100% certain I am providing the knowledge that would see you get there.

Now I know I am one of the only consultants in the Industry that offers this type of Whole Event Extended Guarantee and as you can see, I'm standing behind my products and services – very strongly – by doing it. I can do this because I am 100% certain I'm providing everything I've mentioned and a refund would therefore be a very unlikely circumstance.

While it may seem risky... The way i see it, a lack of guarantee is a bigger sign of an incomplete product or service offering than anything else.

I've also done the same with my Personal Development Company; The Seed of Life. I ran an event with fifty people. I said, "If you feel like I haven't given you over $10,000 worth of value by lunchtime on day one, approach me and tell me and I will refund your money – no questions asked."

Not one person refunded.

What's really interesting about this is, because you set the intention, people find the value because you say, "Hey! This is what it's worth." Because you own it, they pay attention. It's clearly stating... "This is your job. Your job is to find $10,000 worth of value by lunchtime on day one."

What happens?

Because you've set a collaborative intention, you've put that out into the universe. The whole room gets to work on bringing the energy that would be needed to discover this type of value. The universe mirrors it straight back towards you. The power of intention is a fantastic thing.

By offering guarantees, you set what the objective is beforehand and you produce an environment where people are working together towards the common goal. You would be crazy at this point not to try guarantees.

But here is the real kicker and just one more reason why you should try it.

My sales closing percentages when I started implementing guarantees in my business on the phone went from roughly 20 percent to over 45 percent overnight. They more than doubled overnight. Now, if that's not one of the most powerful things you've ever read in any book on business anywhere I'd be a little surprised.

I paid thousands of dollars to learn this. If you use guarantees in your business, you're going to make a lot more money and serve a lot more people with your life changing products and services whilst having a lot more fun.

BUSINESS BREAKTHROUGH QUESTION – What is the result your clients are searching for? If they are completely committed to the actions required to get there; using your knowledge, could you get them this result?

ACTION ITEM – If you answered yes to the question above, you need to structure a guarantee in your business right now. Get onto Law Path or another similar online law service and get a lawyer to put together your terms and conditions with your specific guarantee. Use an e-signing online facility (preferably one with an iPhone or android app so you can make sales without a computer if your need to.) as part of your process; once you have collected credit card details send the contract to be signed electronically.

Key Takeaways From The SALES Section;
(You Fill In Here)

1. ....

....

....

....

2. ....

....

....

....

3. ....

....

....

....

4. ....

....

....

....

5. ....

....

....

Your Business History

List an experience from your past that is explained by the strategies in Sales Section.

....

....

....

....

....

....

....

....

....

....

....

....

....

....

....

....

....

....

List 5 Ideas For New Strategies to Increase Your Sales Conversions;
(You Fill In Here)

1. ....

....

....

....

2. ....

....

....

....

3. ....

....

....

....

4. ....

....

....

....

5. ....

....

PROFIT MAXIMISER # 3; AVERAGE $ SALE

Because 'energy goes where money flows,' the best way to increase the quality of your clients, the results they see, and the utility you both feel, is to charge what you're really worth...

Lets explore...

STRATEGY 9 – What is Your Time Really Worth as An Entrepreneur?

There is an amazing idea I came across in Dan Kennedy's book on No B.S. Time Management for Entrepreneurs. In the book, Dan presents a very polarizing little study.

It starts with the question: "What is your time really worth as an entrepreneur?"

You might be the sole income producer; you might be the key salesperson, the marketer or head of delivery. However it works in the dynamics of your business, adapt and apply the following system to you.

Find a way to make it work.

If we are looking at time, as entrepreneurs, we are at some level trading our time for money. We're also trading our knowledge, which stipulates how much that time is worth. But, at the end of the day, we can only lever up our time, to make it more valuable. At some stage, we will still have to trade our time for money. It's just a matter of what level we are willing to do it.

BUSINESS BREAKTHROUGH QUESTION - "What's your time really worth?"

When I first came across this formula it caused some major earthquakes in my business. I realized, I wasn't extrapolating backwards from my goal. I was just going through the motions. I wasn't reverse engineering, which is often the most efficient way to work something out - to look at the solution and then work backwards.

That's also what i used to do in Math class.

Let's say you want to run a million-dollar-business. It seems to be the goal of a lot of people and, let's face it, I can see why. It's quite a great thing to achieve.

So, you want a million dollars in income. You are the major

income-producer in your business. How do you do it? Firstly we have to look at your time and then we have to look at how much income you're producing now. We've got to break it down hour by hour, minute by minute, to work out if you're going to get there.

Let's assume you work five days a week. So you work roughly 250 days per year. Now, in those days, how many hours do you work? Let's imagine you work ten hours. You work pretty hard. You work 50 hours per week. Now, not all those hours are going to be directly income producing. You're going to have to do some admin. You're going to have to attend occasional meetings. I have banned them in my Business but maybe you still 'need them.' Anyways... You're going to have to do some elements that aren't directly bringing in money.

So, how many hours per day are you bringing in money?

Let's assume 30 percent of your hours – which is quite high; three hours in a day – are directly income producing. If you're looking at this, you're now realizing, "Wow! I only have 750 hours in the year to hit my income goal of a million dollars."

$1, 000, 000.00 / 750 Hours = $1333

If you were to divide a million by 750, you need to make $1,333 on average per income-producing hour to make a million dollars in your business. That certainly puts things in perspective. The first time I ran that exercise I looked at it and thought 'Wow, I'm way off' - and I literally restructured my business the next day. I stopped giving away my time. I lost clients, yes; I lost two of my highest-paying clients, but I was glad to see them leave because they were time vampires who were not getting me closer to my goal, which is fascinating to think about. I prefer working with knowledge vampires.

So, the greatest question to ask is: "Where are you bastardizing your goals right now?" and "How can you delegate anything that's under $1,333 per hour?"

Any hour that you spend not income-producing and trading for design work or sitting in meetings, on social media or doing anything that's not either direct response marketing or sales, is costing you your freedom.

Something else you may have just realised here; you're charging the wrong amount for your products and services.

We're thinking about average dollar sales here. Instead of looking into the greater market and saying, "Oh, what are my competitors charging?" Why don't you look at "What's my income goal for the year? How many hours do I have in the year to achieve it? What are my sales closing percentages? What's realistic for me? Furthermore how much do I need to make per hour? Therefore, what do I need to charge?"

At the end of the day if your business doesn't serve your goals, what's the point? You work hard enough to dictate the terms of how much money you make.

You're in control of your business. Why would you sell yourself into a business that doesn't serve you at the highest level? Find that number, and then go and find a way to serve people at that level. You may not have the resources and the tools and the things you need to sell a product that is $1,000, $3,000 or $5,000.

But as I told you in the previous chapter, everything exists through the process of self-mastery. Just applying and getting results with one of the strategies in this book could be worth a 5-10K offering in your market.

For people saying, "I don't sell products and services more than X," You're simply saying you don't want to grow and therefore you wouldn't make it into my business because, for my goals, I need to serve clients with a growth mindset.

How successful do you really want to become?

If your time is actually worth $1,300, and someone calls you up and says, "Hey Ben, I want a consult with you but I can only afford to pay you $500," do you think that's an option?

You have to think; What's the opportunity cost of all this? You also have to stringently uphold the integrity of your system. Do not step outside of it. This is one of the most powerful strategies I will share with you in the book – optimizing your time, realizing how much it's worth, extrapolating backwards from your goals, and then running Sales and Marketing at an 80/20 ratio.

There is another area of time management we didn't touch on here 'Delegation' - which I will address in Strategy 10, so stay tuned.

ACTION ITEM – Complete the Time Management for Business Owners Exercise

What is Your Income Goal For the Year?

_____

How Many Hours in the Year Do You Have to Complete It? (If unsure go with 750 - 3 income producing hours per day X 250 working days per year)

_____

WHAT IS YOUR TIME REALLY WORTH?

_____

STRATEGY 10 – Why 'Energy Goes Where Money Flows' and How Not Charging Appropriately For Your Products and Services is Destroying Your Business

My brother, Drew, and I used to work in my mum's living room.

Every day, we would meet there. I was living there at the time so I would just wake up, get my stuff, head into the living room, sit down and we would spend anywhere from ten to twelve hours that day, reading, learning and applying the lessons into our online businesses. We were writing blogs, ads, and creating content.

We were paying ourselves $350 a week at that stage of our lives, which was just enough to live off and to train in the gym, which we were very focussed on at that time. All things considered, life was pretty good.

We were intensely focussed on one of our favourite Axioms from Lachlan Cameron, *"Be happy today, whilst striving for more tomorrow."*

Everything started to change the moment that we understood that money was essentially energy. There are a bunch of misconceptions around money, and the process of removing those destructive stereotypes was intensely awakening.

As a result of this perspective breakthrough, we were becoming successful very quickly, and income was rising. We had an online business that was completely automated. We were developing ourselves personally. We had been through Lachlan's course, we'd launched our own program called A Life Worth Living, which I still run today in very limited numbers.

How we sold that program, would teach me one of the most important lessons about the nature of money and business that I have ever encountered. And I've still not heard it repeated outside of this realisation in such clarity.

'A Life Worth Living' was an intensive program, there were over 500 pages worth of materials, videos, exercises, an online membership site, a Facebook group, and weekly coaching calls.

We had originally priced it at $5000.00

However we sold it very differently. We sold 2 people at 5k, two at 3.5K, a couple at 2.5k, one person for 1k and we even let one person slide in for free.

What happened next was absolutely fascinating and has informed everything about what I now do in business. How I charge, how I present my products and services, and how I position myself. What we noticed was the effort and energy brought from the parties who paid the most to be there was considerably higher. In fact it was in direct proportion to the money they spent. Therefore they got a fantastic result. They loved the content. They did every single exercise. They engaged. They were leaders within the community. Frankly, they're still killing it.

One of them has written a book and asked me to write the foreword. How cool is that?

And then, we look at the opposite scale. What happened to the person we let in for free? *"Wow... They got a $5,000 course for free. How awesome for them!"* But, in reality, this person was the one who turned around and said it didn't work...

The others landed exactly where they paid on the graph!

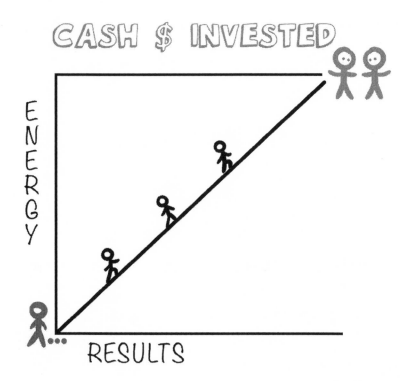

My conclusion around this is; **"Energy goes where money flows."**

If you want to get great results, if you are in the business of changing people's lives and actually helping others, then the more you charge, the better the person's results will be.

This lesson is so profound for your personal finances, and I am speaking from an experiential understanding of this. So it may be hard to intellectualize, however, I encourage you to try it...

The greatest investment you can make in your business is to charge more, because when you do, you are attracting empowered people. When you're attracting empowered people, they turn into fantastic testimonials. And the feedback loop involves people winning on all levels.

The fastest and best way to get the result that you promised, is to charge more, because when you charge, the energy the person shows up with is directly correlated to the money they put down which means they are going to be exponentially more likely to get the result. This applies to health and fitness. This applies to relationship coaching. This applies to a sofa. This applies to absolutely everything.

Think about it. What is the piece of clothing you love most; that you get the most value out of? It also happens to be the one item you paid the most for, right? If you want to be really clever about this, you can use this system to increase your self-worth.

There are three topics here that are all about mindset. It's funny because it's about increasing how much money you're trying to make and how much your products and services are worth.

Your products and services don't become worth anything more. Your perceptions, your beliefs, your enthusiasm is what changes. It's your certainty and your presence that shifts.

I want to tell you a story about a client of mine. I call their gym the 'Messina of gyms' because there's an ice cream store in my hometown Sydney, Australia, that routinely has a line that goes out the door for 50 metres. People come from all over Sydney and when you eat the ice cream, when you go in there, it's an experience. You go, "This is not regular ice cream. I see it now." This is exactly the same as Jungle Brothers Gym, in Sydney. Because Joey and the guys at the gym have built an amazing culture, people can't wait to get in there, and there's a line out the door. So, it's the Messina of gyms.

They have been able to build this for a number of reasons but one is they charge what they're worth. This mirrors back the energy people bring to the gym, and the type of people the gym attracts in general- it's why it is the coolest gym in Sydney. You walk in there and you go, "Wow! This is awesome! There are cool people here. There's cool music. Everyone's doing handstands and swinging on monkey bars. I like it here." The culture in your business starts with how you value yourself.

Here is a small interview with Joey about increasing their prices and seeing what happened off the back of this. Again, this is one of the great paradoxes of business. Most people believe that, by increasing your prices, you're going to push people away. But in reality, you draw the people you want closer, you make a lot more money and they get better results because of it.

How to Successfully Pull off a 33% Price Increase

BEN: Joe... Do you want to give us a bit of background as to who you are and what business you're in?

JOE: I'm Joe Worthington, 32, I'm a gym owner with two of my best mates. We have a business called the Jungle Brothers in Sydney Australia. We've had the gym for a couple of years. It was a very slow start for us. We were pretty fresh with the whole "running our own business" thing.

We started working with you maybe just about seven or eight months ago. Since then, we've experienced a pretty substantial amount of growth in the business but also in our own education and our own understanding of how to run the business.

We've got our space at the moment with 105 members and we have plans to move into a bigger gym.

BEN: One thing I wanted to touch on *that* you guys did - and very well, might I add – You structured a price rise in your business a few months ago. Could you tell us a bit more about it?

JOE: One of the first things you identified was we weren't charging enough for our membership. We were undervaluing our service. We were trying to be competitive with other gyms in the area who have totally different models to ours so it made no sense.

I guess the first part of this process was coming to a mindset shift within ourselves.

And then, in terms of putting it into practice, we structured a whole new membership. We had previously been charging people a fortnightly rate without contract. And so, we built a new model, which was contract-based with a few different price options depending on how long people wanted to commit for.

In conjunction with that, we added some extra services to our products. At the same time, we doubled the amount of classes we had on offer on a daily basis. We introduced open gym hours so people could train here by themselves. We got new client management software which is helping out people to track progress and stay more engaged with their training process. We brought myself on full-time and a few other smaller things.

Essentially, we added these things so we could give more value to our people. And so, then we made a video, which was how we told them about this price rise. We filmed a video – it was my business partner Teora and I talking to the camera.

And so, we had a script – we structured it out in quite a calculated way – we had to express to our tribe that we genuinely want the best for them, we value their patronage, we value their progress, we love them, we want to give them more and we want better results for them. As a result of that, we're putting our prices up because, in reality, if we don't put the prices up, our business just wouldn't stack up in the right way.

It was a little bit of a hard pill to swallow for people and it's a hard thing to ask people to pay you more money all of a sudden. But, at the same time, it was like, "Look, this is the reality of it and we respect you guys and we want you to understand this." We had this faith that, if they are our people, they'll be on-board.

We made the video and we put that into an email with a little bit of text. It was like, "Hey! We've got a really important message. We want you guys to watch it. Check it out." We sent that out and I shat myself.

The next day, I got a phone call from one of our members who was not happy about the price rise. He was like, "What is this? Blah blah blah." I was like, "Oh, no, we messed up! This is the beginning of the cascade of abusive phone calls." And then, that was the only phone call we had.

From there, I got in touch with each member personally. We had told them in the video that the prices would be changing from the month ahead. I think we said, "Look, you've got 20 or 30 days until these price rise is to take effect. By that time, we're going to need to organize your new contract so we'll be getting in touch to sort that out."

Over the course of the next three or four weeks, I had personal phone calls with pretty much everyone. With Teora's help as well... We signed everyone up to new contracts.

The vast majority of people had the opinion of "I totally understand. You guys should have done this earlier. I always thought it was a bit cheap for what you offer," which was like music to our ears. It really reinforced what we were doing. There were a couple of people who were a little bit off-put by it and needed a little bit more convincing but it was fine. Once we had a chance to talk with them and reinforce the reasons why, nobody felt that it was unfair.

That was the process. That probably took us four weeks before we had everyone transitioned on to his or her new membership and that was it.

BEN: Awesome. Well played. What I heard was you structured the price rise but it wasn't just a price rise. It was adding extra value in every area possible. This was essentially a level up in the way you guys do business.

JOE: That's exactly right. It was all part of a bit of a leap forward for us. We did feel like we were undercharging. We should have been charging more initially but we also couldn't put the price up without giving something up top.

BEN: What was the percentage rise in the price?

JOE: The percentages rise, because we went up to a scaled system, depending on their commitment timeframe. It went up on average from 45 to 60 a week.

BEN: 33 percent, yeah that's huge.

JOE: In addition to this, we asked people to enter a contract where they commit for a timeframe which ended up being twofold awesome because we knew they were going to be with us for a longer period of time we were more committed to their results but also they then started to value and respect more what they were doing here because they had financially committed or contractually committed to being a part of this community.

BEN: I love it. So many people would fear that step forward. What were some of the reservations you guys had beforehand... Things you thought might play out?

JOE: We were fearful that we weren't good enough to ask people to pay us more. We thought we had to be competitive with other gyms in our area – 24-hour gyms and stuff. We thought people would just reject the new system because it's not fair or they weren't expecting it.

We were genuinely worried we could destroy our business here. We all felt that but we also recognized we could be destroyed eventually anyway. It felt like, "Pull the Band-Aid off quick. Do it now. Or pull it off slowly over the next six to twelve months and potentially lose a year of your life."

Those fears were real. We had to be constantly reinforcing ourselves that we were worth it and that our members would understand.

BEN: Did you lose any members during the process?

JOE: Yes, we lost two members of fifty at the time. We lost two but it wasn't a direct result of that. The price rise was more of a catalyst for them to reconsider what they were doing.

One of them has since re-joined with us about eight weeks ago. She was put off by the price rise. But then, once we got down into the nitty-gritty of it, it was more that she just wasn't dedicating herself to it and she said, "Look, I'm not going to sign back up just yet but I'll look at it again in the future." She genuinely did. One of the other people said, "Look, I'm going to switch to more of a casual type of arrangement." She buys ten packs of classes, which is another option we have. They were the two human sacrifices, which ended up not being such sacrifices in the end.

BEN: Two people were put off by the price rise but they've come back now and remain to be clients?

JOE: That's right.

BEN: Good result. So, what do you feel like it's been worth to you guys over the six or so months since you have rolled this out? Did you feel like you had to trade any more time, more money or ruin any relationships in the process?

JOE: It's given us a lot more financial freedom. We can now afford to pay ourselves more. We can pay better rates to our outside trainers. We offer more to our people so our relationships have grown. That's a big one. But I think the most important part is that we now really feel like people are respecting our value.

I think it was always a bit of a sore spot for us internally – this battle that we were always fighting to charge less and give more as we thought this was the model to use. When you devalue yourself like that, you don't really do yourself any favours at all, and it's hard to measure the effect of it but it's profound.

Once we were a month into these new sort of membership contracts, I remember the three of us talking about how nice it feels to now be charging what we think we're worth and having this community of people who are truly dedicated and feeling like we had the freedom to give them more. This was a really empowering thing. It's been huge for us. Like I said, It's enabled us to continue building this business that we're so passionate about.

BEN: Awesome. I'm stoked for you guys. Thanks, Joe. I really appreciate your time and the work you guys are doing.

JOE: My pleasure, man. Thank you.

STRATEGY 11 – The Secret to Successfully Upselling At the Time of Order

There is an idea in Behavioural Psychology called the Contrast Principle... It states when we are exposed to two similar things in succession, our perception of the second is altered by our exposure to the first. This is exactly what we're dealing with when thinking about pricing strategy and any other factor involved with positioning or framing an offer. These are the tools available to you as a business owner and it's so important to grasp them.

Have you ever been driving on a highway, You hop off to get some petrol from the nearest town and you realise you are driving 90km in a 50km zone? You didn't do it on purpose but this is the Contrast Principle in action.

At the gym I train at, they have my credit card details on file. And every time I do a PT session, I'd have a great time and, as I was leaving, I would pick up a bar of caffeinated chocolate and take one home.

Because he'd picked up on my pattern, my trainer would say, "Hey, Ben! Do you want one of those? I'll just charge it to the card," What began happening was I came to the PT session and I left with either a bottle of water, coconut water, and a bar of chocolate or all of the above. So I'd spend an extra $10.00 every single time I went in there.

Now, if I had to go up to the counter, pull out my card, and put it on the table and do it the conventional, 'Non Systems For Business Way,' would I have done it every single time? Absolutely not. But did I want the chocolate? Did I want the water? And the coconut water? Yes, absolutely, I did.

There is something important to realise about your nature... We all have an in-built system for not buying the things we want. Once you start to learn this about yourself, you find you're holding yourself back from a lot of chocolate – and other great things you want, and most profoundly... From asking others what they want.

Think of it this way...

There are a lot of people that hate being sold to. But the moment you realize being sold to is a great thing, This is the moment you will become great at sales because what you expect of others is what you expect of yourself. Carl Jung said *"everything that irritates us about others leads us to an understanding of self."*

If you have a repression around what sales means and what they really are, then, of course, you're going to hate being sold to. But, as a business owner you have taken a greater responsibility in the economy and you must own it. Remember the definition I shared with you at the beginning of the sales section:

> *"Selling is getting people intellectually engaged in a future result that's good for them and then getting them to emotionally commit to the actions that would be required to get the result"*
>
> – Dan Sullivan

My favourite retail store in Sydney, Footage, close to an old apartment. I would go there just to get sold because it was the most fantastic selling environment ever. First and foremost, every time I went in there I was treated like a client, and not a customer, and I loved it every single time. It's absolutely fascinating once you recognize these principles.

Something very important to remember about client relationships... Every action or inaction we take is run through a primary filter... "Will this elevate my status?"

Second to this, every time I went in there I was learning, and as I've mentioned information is a beautiful form of leverage. As business owners we need to be perpetual students. Very few things in life can frustrate you when you truly value education and personal development.

You think, *"Oh, how can I go home and apply this to my life and business?"*

You start to appreciate it as a science.

If you buy a car, the upsell done properly occurs once you've pulled out your credit card and agreed to the purchase. The great secret to upselling at the time of order is having the approval to the purchase first. Once they agree to buy, then you offer the extras, because the buying resistance is drastically reduced.

For example, let's say I'm selling an event. I might sell an event for $500 but I have a VIP ticket for $750, which includes a dinner that night, you get to hang out at lunch, and you get private consult.

I might say, "Look, the ticket's $500." They might go, "Awesome! I'm in!" Then I say, "Well, considering you're in, are you interested in upgrading to the VIP ticket which is $750?" You will close a much higher percentage than if you tried to lead with the $750 first. Much higher – I would say 200 to 300 percent higher on the upsell than you would have if you had led with the $750 offer in the first place.

What I'm touching on now is something I teach to my clients called Pricing Strategy. In short, you must strategically test and present your price, in a variety of different ways. What is the best and most effective way of presenting your price? You have to remember, if you are truly selling a life-changing product or service, then you have to do everything in your power to make sure it gets in the hands of as many people as possible and remember, "energy goes where money flows." It's a way to ensure world-class results.

This mindset is one of the most important aspects of business, and it's also extremely rare. If you lead with a marketing and sales mindset it can remove your competition completely. No one else in your market operates with this level of pre-eminence. There's a power in knowing you are going to do everything you can to make sure your prospects and clients get served with what they need. They are under your protection, the client feels it, and responds accordingly.

Many people have a huge repression around marketing and sales. I know because I use to have it myself. "Oh, it's persuading people. Oh, it's negative. Oh, I can't do it!" When, really, marketing and sales is figuring out how to serve people at the highest level and using the skills, strategies, and tactics to go and do just that.

Remember Jay Abraham's Quote, "If you truly believe that what you have is useful and valuable to your clients, then you have a moral obligation to try to serve them in every way possible."

If you can't be on-board with this... I recommend saving the emotional valence and slotting nicely into someone else's business. Just hope they aren't a client of mine because you may find yourself straight back on income generation duties.

When developing your new offers have a think about what your High Return on Investment Offering is?

The second thing is to think about collecting credit card details. If you have clients this means you should be in constant contact because they are under your protection. You should be protecting your clients in the area of life you're serving them in – Which means you should have their credit card details because they should be making repeat purchases.

If you have the credit card details on file, it's pretty easy to go, "Hey, Ben! As you're walking out, I'll charge that to the card." It's good for me because I don't even have to bring my wallet into the situation. Conversational closing is a beautiful thing.

This is one of those tips that I'm giving you in this book. If you play this one alone, depending on what sort of business you're in, this could add anywhere from $10,000 to $100,000 to your business in the next 24 months. So, I'm very grateful to share this sort of knowledge with you and I just hope that you're in the right mindset to apply it.

BUSINESS BREAKTHROUGH QUESTION - How could you conversationally close people within your environment to various products and services?

ACTION ITEM – Insert two potential upsell options *into your sales assets* to strategicallytest after you have made the sale.

ACTION ITEM – Collect credit card details of all new sales from this moment onwards and keep them in a secure and encrypted file.

Key Takeaways From The Average $ Sale Section;
(You Fill In Here)

1. ....

....

....

....

2. ....

....

....

....

3. ....

....

....

....

4. ....

....

....

....

5. ....

....

....

Your Business History

List an experience from your past that is explained by the strategies in the Average Dollar Sale Section.

....

....

....

....

....

....

....

....

....

....

....

....

....

....

....

....

List 5 Ideas For New Strategies to Increase Average Dollar Sale;
(You Fill In Here)

1. ....

....

....

....

2. ....

....

....

....

3. ....

....

....

....

4. ....

....

....

....

5. ....

....

PROFIT MAXIMISER # 4; PROFIT MARGINS

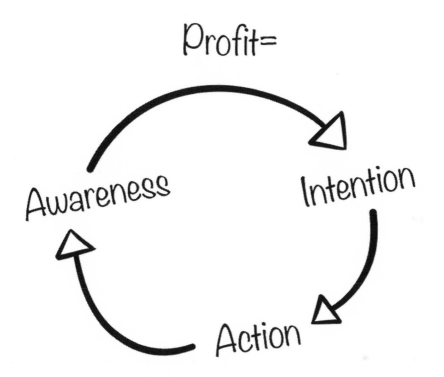

One of the biggest breakthroughs you will ever have in business is the moment you separate Business Income from Personal Wealth Building. First in mind, then through strategy, and finally through implementing action. They are two distinctly separate things. Treat them accordingly and they will continue to serve you.

STRATEGY 12 – Why You Must Blend Physical and Digital Products and Services in Your Business

In our first business, Primal Sydney, my brother, Drew, and I used to fight a lot, because I wanted to be an automated, passive income guy sitting behind the computer. Soon I realized this was an illusion and it doesn't function well in the modern landscape of business.

Drew said to me one day, *"We have to blend physical and digital."* It took me a little while to come around to it. But, after a few months, I saw exactly what he was talking about. I saw that digital sales of our products and services increased after we did a physical event and the sales of our physical events were enhanced off the back of selling them to the people that had bought digital products and services off us.

We came up with a rule; and that rule made us a lot of money. Always blend physical and digital. If you're doing an event, blend something digital after the event. If you're doing something digital, blend an event into it. There are multiple reasons for this and the first and most direct is that you inject your business with connection and emotion.

Maya Angelou once said, "I've learnt that people will forget what you said, people will forget what you did, but people will never forget how you made them feel."

The reason connection is so powerful in business is because of it's link to the memory. I have been blessed in my life to be mentored by, and attend many seminars with, Dr John Demartini.

Here is what John has to say about memories. "Your memory comes in many forms and through your many senses. Any moments that excite your emotional feeling are more likely to be recorded qualitatively than routine experiences"

When you understand how memories and emotions as two inextricably linked parts, you understand to be remembered in business. The best way to do this is to have emotional experiences with your clients.

In the modern landscape of business today, it's easy to want to be a laptop millionaire and hide behind the computer whilst forgetting to inject your brand and your business with one of its most meaningful aspects.

You cannot get the same level of emotional involvement with a purely online program. Physical events always trump them. That's why they produce such better results for clients, and a much larger degree of upsells off the back end.

People like to deal with people. It's a mistake to think business is about removing as much of the emotion as possible. This couldn't be further from the truth.

You are not a cyborg. You are a small business owner and if you're dealing directly with clients, you have to show empathy. You have to inject some sort of compassion into what you're doing.

As a tip... the more vulnerable you can be with your clients, the more vulnerable they will be with you and therefore, the better results you are both going to experience.

As a premise, sit down and look at your business right now.

BUSINESS BREAKTHROUGH QUESTION - "Am I selling physical products or am I selling digital products? How could I enhance the two of those? How could I sell something digital that's going to enhance my physical presence?

Whatever it is, there is some sort of online aspect to what you can do. Perhaps it's a podcast, an information product or a video series – it's really important for your profit margins because, as we've seen in the other module, by selling information, you can achieve huge amounts of leverage. By mixing the two, you lever up the events and you lever up the online presence as well.

For every dollar you make online in your business, you should be making a minimum of $10.00 offline. The only purpose of an 'online businesses' should be to generate leads and to close small sales. Then take your new prospects and clients offline. Offline is where you want to do the majority of your work.

This is the front-end versus the back-end discussion. How do you optimize that? Build your engagement ladder.

My recommendation is that you have an amazing front-end and you lead with a huge amount of value – such as I'm giving you in this book – and then you follow up with a physical event or something tangible. From there, you have options. You can go back into the world of online and do courses and programs. Or you can go back into the world of offline and do more events on the back of that – or a blending of the two. It depends what your unique modality is.

For me personally, I've discovered that my strong suite is speaking at events, rather than online sales or phone sales.

This strategy works both ways too... We've spoken about why it's important to blend physical products and services if you are digital.

But what if you are running a purely physical business?

I had a client a couple of years ago, Tim, who is a podiatrist. He has implemented this strategy with fantastic results. He has a physical presence in the podiatry clinic. He is also a bit of an authority in his specialty. As a result he has developed two online courses. The courses are $300 each. One of those courses is for teaching people how to run properly and the other course is for teaching people how to train their feet and "turn their feet from bricks into springs."

The best thing about all this is... Every single person he sees on a daily basis is a highly qualified prospect for these courses. Because the courses are completely housed in the cloud, they are completely automated, and there's no delivery that needs to be done with them. Once he got past the fixed cost threshold, which was very minimal, it's 100 percent profit, which is very rare in business. I don't know if it's possible to obtain 100 percent profit - without this sort of system.

Think about it this way; Tim doesn't have to spend any more time to make these sales because he is already there working with them. Beyond the first sale, it costs him no more money to make more sales. These sales are costing him no relationship capital and they are clearly enhancing his freedom. This is pure, sweet leverage.

Tim routinely sees anywhere from 20 to 30 patients in a week and he routinely sells up to four to five of these programs per week, which generates an extra $1,500 of income per week.

If you look at this over the space of a year, that's close to $78,000 in extra revenue coming into a business every year just by a small, quick conversation and a mindset that looks to blend physical and digital. Now, if you're a physical business, if you are a hardware, if you are a yoga studio, if you are an accountant or lawyer, you can apply this same strategy.

What's interesting about these scenarios and the information I'm giving you right now – it's life changing, but not everyone implements it. People seem to come up with all the excuses for not having their success.

I was recently consulting with a business trio who run a few gyms, (or physical businesses) in Sydney. They have four locations. After my initial consult, they developed an online course teaching some of their key concepts. They priced it at

$300. Within the first week, they went to work and they sold 15 of those courses within their locations and they made over $4,000.

They conversationally closed these sales into the course. They've already got the credit card details on file. These are the simplest sales to make. Great immediate return on investment. I was very proud to see a client take away a simple idea and turn it into a successful pure profit generating area of their business in such a short space of time.

This is something they can use for the rest of their business's existence, and the lifetime value of each new client that comes into the business has risen significantly.

It's all about taking action.

BUSINESS BREAKTHROUGH QUESTION - "Are You Doing Work That Continues to Work For You?"

ACTION ITEM – Schedule a meeting with yourself or your team... Call the agenda – "Blending Physical and Digital," have a look at what your primary delivery modality is right now, keeping in mind 'what you need is what you don't have,' set new intentions to blend these elements, whilst creating a more highly engaged business in the process.

ACTION ITEM - If you don't already have one, build on online automated course teaching your systems and process you can sell to your clients and prospects. Price it at 10% of the return on Investment they will achieve once they implement the knowledge.

STRATEGY 13 - HOW TO INNOVATE, OPTIMISE, AUTOMATE, DELEGATE And BATCH YOUR PRODUCT DELIVERY

There are three different sections of this chapter. But, first, I'm going to define optimization because this is the Umbrella we are playing under in this chapter.

Optimization is really a form of leverage. It's the answer to...

"How can I improve my process to get more?" Leverage is more of a mindset than anything else, and Ralph Waldo Emerson said it well... "There is always a best way of doing everything."

Innovation on the other hand is the complete shift in strategy... Making the old obsolete.

Through the use of optimisation you can approach Emerson's

philosophy, but never reach it in your business. Because no matter how good you think you've made it, no matter how great things are going, there's always another level.

Emerson also said is his essay on circles, "our life is an apprenticeship to the truth, that around every circle another can be drawn." There's always a new concentric sphere you can push your business into. If you operate from this mindset, it's going to see you grow a lot faster and it's going to see you achieve the things you want in your life.

Optimization is really looking at your results right now and thinking, firstly, "Am I where I want to be?' and, secondly," What are the systems, strategies and tactics I can implement today, tomorrow, and for the next 12 months that are going to help me get to where I need to be?"

For example, you might be sending some online traffic from Facebook to your personal blog, and you might have an opt-in at the bottom of the page. What your'e looking at here firstly; "How much are you paying?" Maybe, one dollar per click, to send the traffic via Facebook? The second question is: "How much are you getting leads for?" or "How many people are opting in at the bottom of the page?" Then you track these numbers to discover "How many of those leads turned into sales and what was the dollar spent per sale?" These statistics are open to optimization.

"Okay. So, I'm making sales for $200.00. How do I optimize that? How do I get it down to $100.00? Do I change the headline? Do I change the copy? Do I change the offer? Do I add social proof elements? Do I add authority elements? Do I do all of the above? Am I making guarantees? What can I do with this?' These are the types of questions you need to be asking, and these strategic enquiries come under the banner of optimization.

What we have covered here is just one example of optimizing for results. However in this chapter I will speak about one of your most valuable assets as an entrepreneur... Optimizing your time.

#1 - Automation

When I was still in the development stage of my entrepreneurial journey – before I'd even started a business – I read Tim Ferriss' 'The 4-Hour Workweek,' a fantastic book. I became aware that I could automate some of the things in my life.

Very early on in the piece, my brother, Drew, and I invested in a piece of software called InfusionSoft. InfusionSoft is a marketing and sales automation software; You can also use to make membership sites and various other things.

With our first business, Primal Sydney – which was a Bodyweight Strength Training Business – we built a completely automated training program that someone could step into, and the system would assess him or her. They take a test, and the system would then filter their results. It would then plug them into their appropriate level and then it would send them all the way through their program from start to finish – completely hands off on our behalf. It did take me about two months to make it. However, after I made it, it was done. It was a 'work that kept on working for me.'

As entrepreneurs, the times you need to be 'on' and 'performing', are incredibly important. One small shift could mean a difference of hundreds of thousands of dollars in income. So it becomes increasingly important as you grow to implement systems underneath you in order to conserve your energy.

A great question to ask under the umbrella of optimization:

"How can I do work that continues to work for me?"

Because, if you're not spending a portion of your day doing work that continues to work for you, or orchestrating work to continuously work for you... You're going to find yourself burnt out, down trodden, and pissed off when things don't go your way. All because you weren't able to maintain the energy you needed to pull things off.

With automation, you are using online systems and platforms to process tasks for you. For it to work, you must firstly deconstruct what you're doing, and/or want to do. Then have a look at all the steps. Finally you inject your thinking process into the computer. You're putting your thought process into the mind of the matrix and then it's going to spit out the desired result every single time like clockwork.

What's really advantageous about this process is that you have to mathematically and scientifically deconstruct what you do. At this point it becomes important to mention... No matter what you're doing – if you're an artist, a painter or you're the world's most pre-eminent esoteric thinker – there is mathematical process behind what you're doing. It's one of the great secrets of the world.

Pythagoras made the infamous quote; "Number is the substance of all things," And the reason he said that is because behind everything, there is science, and behind everything, there is math. Whether it's creativity or not, logic and the logos is still behind it. Creativity is rare math.

And we can use this philosophy in our business. No matter what the task is, we can automate it – which is a big call but it's the truth. If you start stepping into this in your business, you're going to find your time coming back in droves.

You could even delegate your automation work to someone else. Now we're playing.

In the delivery aspect of my business, although I only do two hours or so of delivery a day, I try and spend at least 50 percent of this doing work that continues to work for me – automating emails to go out to clients, automating content and also writing content for them that i only have to write once, and then it continues to live forever. I spend the other 50 percent doing one, one-hour consult per day.

Think of it this way. The work I'm doing right now in writing this book is going to be partially automated once I finish it. I have to do the marketing and the sales, yes, but the delivery? No, I don't have to be there. I don't have to hold your hand, which is true leverage for me and you could consider your education automated. These are the sorts of systems you need to be thinking about applying to your business too.

BUSINESS BREAKTHROUGH QUESTION – "How can you schedule work to continue to work for you and your clients?"

As a caveat to the automation process: Before you automate something, you must optimize it first. If it's got too many steps in it, and it's not optimized to the minimum possible standards, then the automation won't work very well.

First ask, "Okay, is this necessary? How can this be more efficient? How can I get this into a tight little sphere and then automate it from there?"

Get together with your team, your wife, your trusted advisor or your mentor, whoever this person is for you and get the whiteboard out. Have a deep think about what things you can automate in your life right now. Perhaps there is nothing better you could be doing with your time right now.

For example I automate my call booking service with prospective and existing clients. I update my calendar with my available times and then they find a mutually convenient time for the call. In the unlikely circumstance they can't, they let me know.

My favourite piece of automation... I automate a daily email and a daily text message to myself everyday that asks a bunch of specific questions based on what my personal metrics are and what I want to achieve that day. It asks me questions across the seven areas of life.

It asks me questions about my health, my training, nutrition and meditation; it asks me questions about my social life; it asks me questions about touching base with my family; it asks me questions about my personal finance; it asks me a bunch of questions about business because I'm very concentrated in that area; it asks me several intellectual progression questions about how I'm feeling and the work that I've done there, did I read? And then it asks me questions about how I'm feeling intimately and spiritually.

Back to Messages   7:53 AM   ≭ 25%
docs.google.com

HEALTH

The Most Efficient Path to Master Your Psychology is to Master Your Physiology. Train Everyday and Only Eat and Consume the Highest Quality Food and Water.'

DID YOU TRAIN FOR AT LEAST 45 MINS TODAY? *   10 points

○ YES
○ NO
○ Other:

DID YOU EAT 80% HEALTHY FOODS TODAY? *   5 points

○ YES
○ NO
○ Other:

DID YOU FILL OUT THE FOOD DIARY TODAY? *   5 points

◀ Back to Messages   7:53 AM   ≭ 25%
docs.google.com

SOCIAL

'EVERYTHING THAT LEADS IRRITATES US ABOUT OTHERS CAN LEAD US TO AN UNDERSTANDING OF THE SELF'

DID YOU SPEAK TO 1 FRIEND OUTSIDE OF WORK TODAY   5 points

○ YES
○ NO
○ Other:

DID YOU SEND A PERSONAL HANDWRITTEN NOTE OUT TODAY?   5 points

○ YES
○ NO
○ Other:

◀ Back to Messages   7:53 AM   ≭ 25%
docs.google.com

NOTES / THOUGHTS / MUSINGS

HOW DID YOU PERFORM TODAY?

1 2 3 4 5 6 7 8 9 0
○ ○ ○ ○ ○ ○ ○ ○ ○ ○
HORRI   GREA
BLY   T

WHAT WAS ON YOUR RADAR TODAY? - ANY QUOTES / STORIES / THOUGHTS YOU WANT TO SAVE?

Your answer

WHAT DO YOU NEED THAT YOU DON'T HAVE?

ANYTHING YOU NEED? *

Your answer

At the end of that, I fill in all of the details. I get a score out of 100 that gets sent to my phone. I call it 'The Seed of Life Score.' And what I've noticed is that; in the days I succeed in business are the days that I show up in every single area of my life and nothing can hold me back from that.

I also reset the survey every month to be in more alignment with my monthly goals and what I'm trying to achieve that month.

This took me less than an hour to set up. It arrives every day at 7:30 p.m. I get sent my text. It costs me less than $0.10 and it's absolutely invaluable to my personal development. I'm playing a game against myself and I want to win. Every day, I want to win the game. "Can I get 100 out of 100 today?" I've never gotten it. I hope to one day but maybe I won't, it's a challenging test.

This is an excellent example of a simple automation that adds a bunch of value to my life and saves me a bunch of time. I'm using InfusionSoft to do that for me.

#2 – Outsourcing

Outsourcing is using online platforms – such as Upwork, Freelancer, etc - to post a job online and get someone from India, Pakistan, the Philippines, or somewhere where there's cheap labour to do your tasks at drastically reduced costs. You are using economies of scale.

This is really powerful as a small business owner. If you're not using it, then you should definitely get on it. I personally use Upwork. I think it's excellent. I don't have an affiliate for link this – maybe I should – but, it's an excellent system and it works well. The money is put in escrow so it's safe, you only pay at completion of the job and you can post any type of job. You can post a job for transcription services, design work, accounting tasks, automation tasks, just about anything you want.

As a personal example, for this book, for each chapter, I recorded myself having a little monologue, or a podcast – you can imagine – and I sent that to an upworker and they transcribed it for me. When it came back, I then edited it and I put it into the book. This saved me a bunch of time. It would have taken me ten to twenty times longer to write this book had I not outsourced this transcription service.

BUSINESS BREAKTHROUGH QUESTION - What can you outsource in your business? What is your budget?

I spent $250 (AUD) to get this entire book transcribed. Do you think that's a worthwhile investment for me?

Have a think about what elements in your business can be outsourced? Write a list of them. What are the things that you've been meaning to do? You can think design, transcriptions - just about anything you want besides marketing and sales.

RED FLAG - Never outsource marketing and sales in your business until you have mastered it.

I was speaking to an ex-client recently (this relates to the next strategy of delegation), and he told me that he insists on delegating his sales. Within that exact moment, I foresaw him experiencing a completely self-inflicted sabotage. And in that moment, I knew he was about to go through one of the biggest self-sabotage attempts I've ever seen in my life. And I knew that he was no longer going to be a client of mine. Looking to outsource sales before you have mastered it is running away from the work of essential growth.

In reality he wanted to outsource sales and marketing because he had 'sales fear'. People become very irrational when under fear, which is perfectly normal, but in life it's how we respond to the stimulus we receive that defines the lives we lead. He chose the wrong path and stood by it ignorantly.

As a business owner, I urge you not to outsource marketing and sales – unless you're marking over $1,000,000 a year, and you know everything there is to know about marketing and you know everything there is to know about sales. Even then, I would not recommend it. Prior to cracking 7 figures, you simply should not do it because you will never learn the systems of how to generate a lead and how to close a sale; which are the two most financially empowering studies you will ever undertake in your life.

Remember, going through the void is the only way to create something of value. Don't rob yourself of efficiency, accountability, productivity, and the freedom you could obtain by understanding these simple business philosophies at a deep level.

A simple mathematic understanding puts you in the position of authority over your financial security. But, if you don't understand marketing and sales, trust me when I say your money will be best spent coming to my seminar where I teach it to you. If you're unaware of what the sales and marketing process really means, you will never know what to expect once you do outsource it, which is the big issue. Please take that on-board.

Never outsource marketing and sales without an extremely legitimate reason for doing so.

#3 – Delegation

The last tool is delegation. Even I have a hard time implementing this imperative task. Ever since I was little, I played rugby union. I grew up playing in a region of Sydney that was tough. At about 10 years old, I was playing against well-developed, heavy-set Island natives, weighing well over 100 kilos (that's slightly over 220 lbs).

When there was a penalty, each team lined up with 10 meters in-between - and one team would get the ball. Then I'd have 100KG+ of body mass running my direction full speed, trying to crush me.

As young as I could remember, I was always the first person off the line to go and tackle that 100kgs of body mass. I don't know why. I think it was something my dad instilled into me when I was very young, as he actually encouraged me to partake in this sort of behaviour.

This is probably why I have reached a level of success in business, but it's also something that holds me back, because at a very young age I have commonly decided to take other people's fears and frustrations and run with it because I have a high pain threshold.

In business, that's really great. But at times I find myself doing menial tasks. I do it all myself because, sometimes, I just think it's easier that way. I am acutely aware that what got me to where I am, isn't going to get me where I'm going. And though, I may not be a master at delegation, I do consciously acknowledge it. I need to improve my skills in this area.

In strategy 9 we discovered how much your time is now really highly valued. And if your time is now worth – and it might be $500, it might be $600 – you have to think about delegation, because you now have an obligation, and permission, to delegate anything under that. This is a new mindset, which can accelerate your growth when done properly.

I'm not pretending to be a master at it. However at this stage, I thought it appropriate to make you aware of it, and myself more accountable for fixing it. This is one strategy we need to work through together and I may need some support as well as we go through this.

STRATEGY 14 - SYSTEMATICALLY CUT DOWN ON USELESS EXPENSES - AND GET STAFF INVOLVED IN INCOME PRODUCING WORK

What follows is the least sexy chapter of this whole book. Therefore, it was the last chapter I wrote. Though many of the chapters are about the increases, this one is about the decreases. It would be a little rude not to mention it because it has some profound implications, and though it may not be as exciting, it has an equal capacity and the ability to improve your profit margins - so it's something we need to address.

You need to cut down on useless expenses.

Without going into too much depth on the philosophy of why we should do this, it's more about the actions. Print off all of your expenses for the past 12 months. Put them down in front of you with a highlighter, and highlight anything that is not essential to the day-to-day marketing, sales, and delivery of your process. By "essential" I mean; what is the relationship between this element and income generation? And secondly, is there a cheaper, better, more effective way of doing this specific task?

BUSINESS BREAKTHROUGH QUESTIONS;

- Are these 'expenses' directly involved in income generation?

- If yes - Is there anything that will do the same job to the same level of proficiency, that is cheaper, better or more effective?

What you'll find is you have a bunch of applications – especially if you're in the world of online business. You'll have a bunch of applications that are all doing the same thing; as I did the first time that I performed this exercise.

I had thousands of dollars per month in subscription services to various applications, because I felt I needed these separate applications to run particular tasks. It just snowballs out of control. In reality, if you just refocus onto the things that matter and stay away from the bright, shiny objects, you're going to run a more efficient system. This is what the 'Systems For Business Philosophy' is all about.

A mentor of mine once said to me: "When money appreciates, it appreciates." I think that's exactly what we're talking about here. Once you appreciate where you're spending your money and don't be so nonchalant about it, you become certain that you're making investments, and your income tends to rise.

I believe spending money on nice quality clothing and spending money on Mont Blanc pens, notebooks and various other quality things, is ultimately going to help you in business, and are therefore investments. But spending money on random applications you think you need just because everyone in your market is using them, is converse to this rule.

If you're paying staff – and here's where it gets very exciting – *** all staff in your business should be focused in some way on marketing and sales. If you would like to employ someone to do delivery, that's fine, but make sure you find a way for that person to pay back their wage every week. Every single person in the business should make the minimum of their wage back in direct marketing input or sales results. That's a rule that you should apply to your business, because you move your staff from 'expenses' to 'investments'. You never have to worry about paying your staff again because you have reached arbitrage. And we love arbitrage.

This is a simple strategy to implement. Take one of their days – if they're a full-time staff member – and get them focusing on marketing and sales. Set the quota in the day for double the amount of money you need to pay them for the week and make sure they hit this. If they don't perform, educate them more. Link what they are doing to their highest values. You will never have to worry about paying that staff member ever again.

BUSINESS BREAKTHROUGH QUESTION - Where in your business can you map over existing expenses to investments?

Can you map everything over in your business to marketing and sales? We've spoken about how you can do that with your time in the 80/20 principles. But, with a simple shift in strategy, and shift in mindset towards marketing and sales within your business, the effects will be profound.

It's also important to lead with reward. Pay your staff appropriately for the work they do on marketing and sales. Give them extra commissions, because if they make money above the quota everyone wins. Once they master it, they will likely love their increased freedom so much they will be begging to make more income for you.

Most people live their lives within a sticky situation I call a double bind or a gordian knot. They find themselves in a situation. Then they turn around, and they're in the corner. They're backed up. They're scared. They're frustrated. They're fearful. And then they realize, "Well, I've got two options. I can either go right or I can go left. But, if I go right, this negative thing is going to happen; if I go left, this equally negative thing is going to happen."

The echo of indecision starts ringing.

A double bind – *when* every area you perceive you can go is negative.

I like to orchestrate double binds in business and so too in the other 6 areas of my life. No matter where I go and no matter what I do, every single element will turn into growth for me. By understanding the dynamics of growth in health, human behaviour, entrepreneurship, personal finance, marketing and sales, you too can achieve this in your life.

From my mentors I have learnt, **the master transmutes everything they are going through and knows there's no failure, there's only feedback; for the master there are no double binds.**

You could run the same strategy in your business. If you perceive there's an expense, then you're not looking at it properly and you're not optimizing it appropriately. Could you map over all of your expenses and turn them into investments and see what happens to your business?

Key Takeaways From The Profit Margins Section;
(You Fill In Here)

1. ....

....

....

....

2. ....

....

....

....

3. ....

....

....

....

4. ....

....

....

....

5. ....

....

....

Your Business History

List an experience from your past that is explained by the strategies in the Profit Margin Section.

....

....

....

....

....

....

....

....

....

....

....

....

....

....

....

....

List 5 Ideas For New Strategies to Increase Your Profit Margins;
(You Fill In Here)

1. ....

....

....

....

2. ....

....

....

....

3. ....

....

....

....

4. ....

....

....

....

5. ....

....

PROFIT MAXIMISER # 5; AVERAGE PURCHASES PER YEAR

I would like you to imagine you're standing at a machine right now, and there is one slot there... You can insert a $100 bill and every time you do $200 comes right back out.

How often would you play?

STRATEGY 15 - The Truth About 'Irresistible' High Return on Investment Offerings

There's three separate ways to run a small business.

ONE; You can run a business selling commodities, which is the silliest way to run a small business, and could be correlated to what our version of hell might look like.

TWO; You're business can run a price strategy. You put your costs up all over the place and you never communicate the return on investment.

THIRD; and, really, the only strategy you should be running as a business owner, (especially if you're a business-to-business space,) is a value-based business formatted around the *Return on Investment Offering.*

In the mind of any prospect, there are three possible outcomes. When they put something down on their credit card, with their savings, or in cash, they are thinking either...

1. **Cost**
2. **Price**
3. **Or Investment**

The cost is for commodities. The price is what it's going to take from them to get the result. And the investment is where they will be at some point in the future once they make the order.

It's your job to answer the predominant thought in the mind of any prospect...

"What's in it for me?"

People don't buy products and services, they buy results. You need to meet them there and communicate how them spending quantities of their time, money, efforts, energy, resources, relationships, freedom, and any other allocation you'll be asking them for – how them spending those qualities and quantities is going to equal more of them on the other side. It doesn't have to be financial either. It's great if it is though, as long as there is a clear and communicated path they can clearly see. This will see you grow a wildly profitable business.

There is a great old advertising story...

Two men approached, each offering a horse. Both made the same claims. The horses were gentle, kind, and would be suited to a daughter. The first stated, "try the horse for a week, if you don't like it I will refund the money." The second "try the horse for a week for free and if you like it come and pay me then."

Naturally you choose the second horse.

Let's imagine you are in a coaching business and you sell mindset coaching. It's excellent that you sell mindset coaching. However, most mindset coaches don't communicate the value of what they're doing and they rarely map it over to an increase in financial health. As you may be aware, a predominant thought in the mind is 'financial health'.

Could you use your products and services to guarantee this result? If you can't guarantee the result, then why would people continue buying off you? We're talking about average purchases per year here; This is one of the greatest secrets in business.

'The Systems For Business Philosophy' states, If you can generate a return on investment from your offerings, every time someone buys something off you, they are standing at a machine cashing in as they make more money, they get more time, they get more relationships, they get more freedom, they get more resources. They're going to keep buying because this is arbitrage we're talking about here. One dollar in, two dollars out...

These people are going to continue the relationship. They're going to give you more referrals. They're going to keep coming back!

As an example, in my business, for businesses over the 1 Million Dollar Mark, I offer a return on investment that I will increase your net profits in 24 months or less, without spending any more time, ruining relationships, running away from your purpose, or doing anything you don't want to do – or it's completely free.

Do you think that's a pretty good return on investment for a 7-figure business owner? What do you have to lose? This is because I need to make sure I am serving you at the deepest level. If I'm not, then what's the purpose of my business? If I'm not focussed on helping you, what's the point? If I'm not listening to what you want, then, I may as well sell a commodity.

Make sure your business is selling something in the marketing or the sales space, which are two excellent spaces to be in because they are focused primarily on financial returns on investment. If you don't have those sorts of offerings in your business and you sell business-to-business, how could you structure this?

Could you have a marketing and sales aspect to your business? Even if you're a "branding business", or a "designer", master marketing and sales in your own business. Once you've mastered it, sell it back to others and then do design, marketing, and sales. That's a much more powerful business because you have just moved your services from cost to investment.

If you cannot trace a clear and direct line from design to marketing to sales, then you are not looking hard enough. You are literally devaluing yourself. And I cannot help you. That is going to be the evolving state of the business owner today because we're in the age of information. Why should I choose to tell you exactly what to do with the design, and then go and connect it to my marketing myself, and then go and connect it to the sales? You would make ten to a hundred times more money if you drew that line yourself. It's the same for all business.

A predominant thought is: "How can I make more money?" If you understand that, it means you are helping your clients to create what they want. Therefore, they can continue to pay you, which is obviously what we all want.

As a tip on this, sell continuity. What do I mean by that? I sell courses and programs and products that are on a month-by-month continuity basis. You might sell a $2,000 per month consulting package for twelve months. Or you might sell it at $1,000 per month. What level do you want to play at?

If it's not working for you, then it's pretty clear you're not generating a return on investment for your clients. Don't throw it out. Go back to the drawing board and think, "Okay, how can I generate the return on investment my clients are looking for? Therefore, they're going to continue to pay me." Therefore, your lifetime value of a client shoots up rapidly.

Now, if you're in the business-to-consumer space, let's say that you're a jeweller; the same rules apply. What is the predominant goal, the predominant thought, in the mind of your clients? If you don't know, go and ask them. What are they looking to achieve?

In relation to finding out what your "Irresistible High Return on Investment Offer" could contain. I have found the following to be an excellent question. It comes from a guy called Dan Sullivan. (I've restructured it a little for this situation)

"So, John, I'd like to imagine we're sitting together. It's twelve months' time. We've done some work together. And you have been taking all the actions on the back of your newfound knowledge, and/or product. At the end of that twelve months, what are you and I celebrating?"

This question is so powerful because - you pre-frame that they've done the work with you, you pre-frame they've shown up to continue the actions required to get the result, and you've pre-framed exactly where they see themselves. In this moment, they're going to tell you what their return on investment is. Then, you do everything in your power to make sure they achieve the result, and then as we discovered in strategy 8, you guarantee it.

If they're willing to make the commitment to action, you can guarantee it. Therefore, you can drastically increase the average price of your services because you focused on Return On Investment, and once they achieve the result as a result of your process you have a client for life. They will purchase again and again. (Also they are more likely to refer, and you can use their casestudy video in your marketing)

BUSINESS BREAKTHROUGH QUESTION – What is the tangible return on investment from doing business with you? Is this anywhere in your marketing? This is more important than your products and services...

ACTION ITEM - If the question above is not in your sales process you need to get it in there. This one simple question has the power to drastically increase your sales conversion percentages, because you will have found and focussed in on your tangible return on investment.

ACTION ITEM – Become a perpetual student of marketing. Start researching offers. Read ads and patrol Facebook. Become aware of a few more of these 5000 messages. What works and what doesn't. Why have you bought before? Ask others.

STRATEGY 16 – Discover the 4 Quadrants of Scale

There's a great scene in the movie Fifty Shades of Grey.

And don't ask me why I was watching the movie... It may be because I was locked in a house in Patagonia Argentina, working on this book for three weeks.

In the scene, the protagonist who is a sex fiend says to the lady, "Do you trust me?" She looks at him in the eyes and says, "Yes, I trust you." And then, he proceeds to tie her up with a bunch of medieval-looking apparatus' and blatantly have his way with her for the next ten to fifteen minutes of the film...

Now, I'm purely using this as an example, I'm not suggesting you tie up your clients. But I am suggesting the power of trust can be a powerful business asset.

Trust in business is the most valuable asset you can acquire, and it can be acquired. Trust predates everything. There's a great quote from Zig Ziglar. He said, "Nothing happens until the sale is made." Yes, I agree with Zig, but we could extrapolate that one step further and say, "Nothing happens until trust is built," because there is not one single sale that is made without trust.

For this I turn to my "know and trust" matrix. It divides the four potential client and prospect segments in your business and, therefore, the four potential income streams in your business.

THE KNOW / TRUST MATRIX

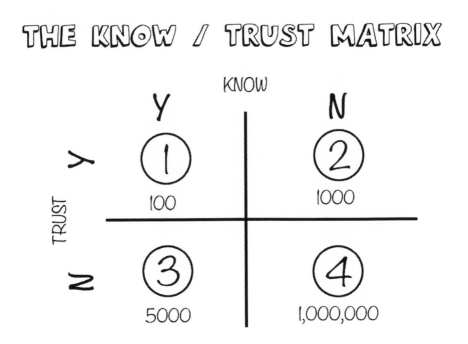

KNOW

	Y	N
Y	① 100	② 1000
N	③ 5000	④ 1,000,000

TRUST

In the top-left quadrant, Quadrant 1, you have people who know you and trust you. This is most commonly your highest performing clients. Underneath this, in Quadrant 2, you have people who don't know you, but they trust you. Now, how could someone not know you but they trust you?

You have borrowed the trust of another person by using Strategic Partnerships.

If you've got Quadrant 1 – people who know and trust you – What you could do is borrow the trust of those people and get them to speak on your behalf, or to endorse you, or to become an affiliate for you, or to become a strategic partner with you. You can therefore reach new prospects who you don't know but acquire a high level of their trust. This is why, in my lead generation strategies, number two is strategic partnerships. It's one of the best ways to build a business.

Now, we move up to Quadrant 3, we've got people who know you, but they don't yet trust you. This could be thought of as the world of Facebook, or the world of online marketing or all of your prospects on Facebook.

And then, in the bottom-right-hand corner, Quadrant 4, you've got people who don't know you and don't trust you. They've never heard of you before, they don't know who you are, and they don't trust you. They wouldn't be interested in you if I were to mention your name.

If we're thinking from Quadrant 1, to 2, to 3, to Quadrant 4... I also like to think of this as warmth. In Quadrant 1, this person is extremely warm towards you. In Quadrant 4, this person is extremely cold towards you. They're moving through a spectrum. And it's your Job to accelerate, wield, and orchestrate this process.

THE SALES SPECTRUM

COLD   WARM   HOT

It's simply much easier to make a sale further up the warmth, and towards the hot spectrum, than it is down towards the cold spectrum. The issue with this is that the majority of business owners focus the majority of their time, efforts, energy, and resources on cold prospecting – on trying to build trust with a cold audience. Most of the time they are not even building trust; they are trying to sell them. Which is a big no, no under the Systems For Business Philosophy.

The engagement ladder in a previous section is all based off trust and rapport. You're moving people through the cold to the warm with information, then you're moving them from the warm to the hot with some sort of highly engaging, and trust building, product or service that's a little bit lower end, then you're moving them towards the hot, and then to the steaming, piping hot within an event or a program or a course.

Now if I'm working or consulting with a business and they come to me with a cash flow problem, I immediately use this matrix and I look at: What are your assets in Quadrant 1? I look there first. The reason I look there first is because it's exponentially easier and faster to work there than it is in Quadrant 2, 3, and 4. Why would you make things harder for yourself? As hard as business already is, why would you make it harder for yourself by jumping into 2, 3, and 4, if you don't have to?

After I've addressed Quadrant 1, then, I step down to Quadrant 2 and look at what assets we might develop there. Then I step down to Quadrant 3, and then finally I step down to Quadrant 4.

Something to note here also is; all the quadrants are equal in benefits and drawbacks. They have different levels of difficulty however they're still equal because each quadrant has a different level of scalability.

Think of it like this: You only have a certain amount of people in your life who know you and trust you. It's a finite quantity. Let's say there are a hundred people in your life who know you and trust you. Then, how many people do they know? How many people know them and now trust you? Let's say they know a hundred people each, and maybe they're only willing to refer 5. Well, if we're looking at a hundred people and then we times it by 5, we're looking at 500 people.

There are 100 people in Quadrant 1. If you're a top performer there are maybe 1000 people in Quadrant 2. Now, in Quadrant 3 – people who know you and don't trust you – you might be looking at about 1000-5000 people – it depends how big your online audience is. In the bottom-right-hand quadrant... How many people don't know you and don't trust you? There's 7 billion of those, but once you niche down to your dream client maybe 1 million – 2 million people.

Each specific quadrant has its advantages and disadvantages of going after. One of them is easier and faster, yes, but you're going to expel this resource a lot faster too. You cannot build a business by purely targeting people who know and trust you. Well, I guess you can if you're developing seriously high return on investment offers and you're continuously building rapport and building value and helping them make money. However, I have found it's best to do all of them at the same time, and dig your well before you're thirsty. In other words, when the times are good; focus on the harder sales to make. When times are tough ease up the difficulty, to build income and confidence.

The greatest asset towards scalability is targeting people who don't know and don't trust you. However, the greatest asset towards existing profitability and increasing the lifetime value of your client – not the amount of clients you have but the lifetime value of each client – is to target Quadrant 1 and Quadrant 2.

In a business run under the Systems For Business Philosophy your clients are your most qualified prospects.

One of the smartest questions to ask yourself regarding business is; "How can I develop products and services to continuously serve my existing clients to at the highest level?" By association, this implies you have to apply all of the other strategies we have discussed in this book.

You cannot run this strategy if you're not developing return on investments for your clients. You cannot run this strategy if you do not have an engagement ladder. You cannot run this strategy if you are not excellent at sales and marketing.

As you're probably seeing through the nature of this book, the way it's evolving and the way that I've intentionally formatted it, all of these strategies begin to work together as one and work towards the common goal. They all touch each other; they leverage off, and add to each other.

I call this Geometric Thinking – You achieve it by applying multiple vectors, multiple points of leverage to each thought, situation and circumstance in your business. You could ask... "How can I be improve my service? Who can I be serving more?

How can I make more sales? How can I serve this person at the highest level possible?"

Once you master this level of thinking I'm intending to implant into your brain, you're going to have one of the greatest keys to business success for the rest of your life.

By applying the 'Know and Trust Matrix,' you should never develop products and services for people who don't know you and don't trust you before you've developed those services for people who know and trust you. They're right there in front of you. Just ask them what they want. Literally, it's that simple. You can ask them what they want and they will tell you.

Then, you can assume that there are more people like them and then step down to Quadrant 2.

You could approach it like this...

BEN; "Hey, John! You really loved the program I just created for you. Would be interested in telling some of your friends about it? If you do, I'll give you 50 percent of the income from any of the sales I make. How does that sound?"

JOHN; "Well, that sounds awesome Ben! I may end up profiting off the product that you sold me."

BEN; "Yes, that's exactly right! Actually, you'll end up making way more money than you paid me for it. Therefore, you'd get it for more than free. That's a pretty good deal, isn't it?"

Once you have case studies saying how amazing the product is, you have your social proof and you can move into quadrant 3 and 4.

And that's because, you're not standing there righteously proclaiming...

"Hey! Look at me! How awesome is my product?" But instead,

"Here's what John has to say about the amazing transformation he just went through." This immediately builds trust.

By using this sort of strategic marketing your prospects will jump voluntarily into Quadrant 1 and they will become exponentially easier to sell.

So to recap; By following, you've built more of an income base by serving people at a higher level. You've probably made a ton of profit because you haven't spent lots of money on marketing. You have used Leverage.

What you could do is use that income to inject into a sales and marketing campaign, that is targeted towards people who don't know you and don't trust you – which will be more of a longer sales cycle, therefore costing you a little bit more money.

Once you crack this, hit it with it's full weight to find scalability in your business.

BUSINESS BREAKTHROUGH QUESTION – Who am I targeting right now with my marketing? Am I shooting myself in the foot by making things harder than they need to be?

ACTION ITEM – List out your 'Know and Trust Quadrants' and the participants that live within. Develop 4 separate marketing campaigns with separate strategies and intentions to target each specific Quadrant.

Key Takeaways From The Average Purchase / Year Section;
(You Fill In Here)

1. ....

....

....

....

2. ....

....

....

....

3. ....

....

....

....

4. ....

....

....

....

5. ....

....

....

Your Business History

List an experience from your past that is explained by the strategies in the Average Purchases Per Year Section.

....

....

....

....

....

....

....

....

....

....

....

....

....

....

....

....

List 5 Ideas For New Strategies to Increase the Average Number of Purchases Per Year (You Fill In Here)

1. ....

....

....

....

2. ....

....

....

....

3. ....

....

....

....

4. ....

....

....

....

5. ....

....

PROFIT MAXIMISER # 6; AVERAGE YEARS CLIENT STAYS

"History is, in large, a battle of the minorities, the majority applauds the victor and provides the human material for social experiment"

–Will Durant

Let's build your CULT-ure...

STRATEGY 17 - How to CREATE A TRIBE MENTALITY

The first element of building a tribe is believing in what you do.

Seth Godin, in his amazing book, said, "The secret to leadership is simple – do what you believe in, paint a picture of the future, go there, and people will follow."

Out of all the human behavioural theories in this book, this one presents so much power because as human beings we have a built-in drive to be connected. We have an built-in drive to want to be a part of something.

You only have to look back into history to see there has been a battle of minorities. We form these little sectors; we form into groups to stand for something, to believe in something. It's how we build our identities. It's how we tap into our purpose. To not use this tool in your business is really quite silly.

There are an amazing couple of books by an author called Robert Cialdini, and I believe the systems and theories in his books are the most profound theories you can find in the area of persuasion, and therefore marketing and sales.

In one of Robert's books he talks about a study where they ran two separate tests. The first one was when people approached their clients and asked, "Hey! I'm looking for your opinion on this." They're looking for a collaborative sort of input from the clients in the business.

What they noticed is that, when they asked for an opinion, people took a half step backwards. But, when they reframed that language and changed the framing of the question to: "Would you be interested in giving us some advice?" people took a half step forward and were more receptive to give positive feedback.

This is so instrumental when we're thinking about tribes and tribe mentality. When we feel like we're a part of something, we support and we help to create.

There's an old saying, "People don't sink the boats that they're in." And you may be the captain of your ship but your clients and prospects are the crew and they are right there paddling with you. They are driving you to become the leader – to push forward with your ideas, advice and to charter new territory.

So with this in mind… How do you build your tribe? Your CULT-ure?

Will Durant in his epic 13-part, over 10,000 page series of books 'The Story of Civilization,' came to the conclusion; "History is in large the battle of the minorities; The majority applauds the victor and supplies the human material for social experiment"

So first of all, we have to stand for something. And we have to stand for something on the edge because this is the only way our message will ever provide people with more meaning in their lives.

Two of the major themes running through every single strategy I've shared with you in this book are; emotional connection and empathy. And as the leader of your tribe, as you're starting a tribe, one of the best ways to gain momentum is to take a stance against something and use this to push yourself forward.

For example, I have a client who is a podiatrist. He takes a stance against orthotics, the general way in which podiatry is done, and he's building a great tribe around this.

I have another client who is a gym owner and they're taking a stance against 'Globo' Gyms and the conventional ways of doing fitness, and they're making it more fun. They're making it more about movement and they've built an amazing tribe. I went to their Christmas party and it was one of the best moments of 2016 for me. Looking around there, you could sense and feel the tribe mentality – They've truly mastered it, better than anyone else i've seen. It's because they're standing for something, something you get to be a part of.

You're in their boat, with the oar in your hand.

Another thing to consider; each member you add to your tribe is compound interest. How much more likely are you to get referrals when you run the tribe mentality? How much more likely are people to stick around when you run the tribe mentality? How much more likely are they to spend money to be there? This is more than just training. This is more than just business. People feel it... This is something we're called to be a part of and we want to inject ourselves into.

Aristotle said, "To avoid criticism, say nothing, do nothing, be nothing."

And as the leader of your tribe, you have to expect people to try to take it away from you. People will try and chunk you down. It is said that the greatest general is the one who is seared in battle scars. And looking back at Aristotle's quote, if you want to become something meaningful, you must expect criticism. Expect people to try and take it away from you because, for any idea in the world, there will always be the opposite idea.

It's universal law and there is no escaping polarity. So best to just prepare for it.

If you take a stance, if you start to build a tribe, another tribe will eventually try and attack you. As the leader, as the business owner, you have to stand firm and stand hard.

Jay Abraham once said, "people are silently begging to be led" and this is a great secret in business – stand for something. Do not care what others think, care about what your tribe wants. The greatest general is seared in battle scars.

BUSINESS BREAKTHROUGH QUESTION – Does your market segment have their own language? Are you using this in your marketing?

BUSINESS BREAKTHROUGH QUESTION – Can you coin original language to communicate with your tribe?

STRATEGY 18 - The Secret Gift That Keeps on Giving… And Keeps Them Staying

This one item I have given my grandmother, and I've given this gift to both my Grandmother, and my Mother.

When I gave it to my Grandmother, she told me she was going to take it to the grave with her. Which may sound quite morbid but if you knew my Nanna you would see it quite funny. She also wrote back to me the story of her life in a notebook and gave it to me as a gift – which is one of the greatest gifts I've received in my life.

The gift I gave my mother, which was this same gift, is still on the fridge in her house close to six months later, after her birthday. I don't see any other birthday cards still on the fridge from that year.

Now, this same thing – as ridiculous as this may sound – is one of the most powerful things I've ever applied to business, the Personal Handwritten Note; it could also be a note, a letter, or a postcard. What is important is that it's something with your physical, handwritten presence on it. This is key. It must be handwritten. It's likely one of the most emotionally powerful and simply authentic gestures that you can ever make.

Have you ever received a Personal Handwritten Note? How did it make you feel? If you haven't received one before, you can still get involved... Try writing one to someone else - this feels even better.

You only have to look at the two examples I've just given you to know what this means for someone when you reach out and authentically share what you really feel, and offer your deepest thoughts and vulnerabilities.

In business, it's easy to want to remove the emotional aspect of everything we do. It's easy to want to make it purely rational and steer clear of your vulnerabilities as you hide behind your logo.

However... I have seen the opposite to be more effective. I am certain the secret to great business – is vulnerability.

To second that point, the secret to mastering vulnerability is that you can only share things once you've transcended them and once you've found gratitude for it. Don't be vulnerable whilst you're in the pit. You can only be vulnerable once you've found the growth in your pain. People don't want to hear the trials and tribulations. People only want to hear your struggle when it comes with the boon.

I've always had an affinity for the Personal Handwritten Note, because I experienced it at a young age. When I was 12 years old, I made my first grand final. Our coach Brian was a father of one of the guys on my team, he also happened to be a professional rugby coach.

On the day of the Grand Final he gave us all personal handwritten notes...

Here's what mine said...

"I have given you all the skills you need – Don't look for me on the sideline, I will be in the stands enjoying the game. Play as a team, remember your basic skills, back yourself and your teammates."

We won that Grand Final and I have never forgotten the power of a handwritten note.

I heard about the personal handwritten note a few more times. It popped up on my radar again at a Mal Emery seminar in Sydney, Australia. And again a third time I heard it on the I Love Marketing Podcast, from a guy named Steve Sims.

They both said the same thing. They said that the personal handwritten note was the most underutilized aspect of business. In the modern world of online marketing and business, the world of technology and the world of information we live in a lot of our human connection has been stripped away from us.

But, as I told you earlier in the book, memories are enhanced with emotion. And the emotion contained within reaching out to someone and writing a personal handwritten note is profound.

It is so far beyond writing a Facebook post, an email, or anything online – even if it took you the same amount of time. The prestige behind physically writing something is exponentially greater than writing something via the web, or sending a digital meme.

The physical result of getting it in your hands seeing the time someone put into pushing their pen to paper, that's what's it's about. You can touch it. You can feel it. It adds power to your message.

I've always been someone that's written notes and letters to people. I've always been really interested in it – mainly because I've loved receiving them. Whenever I've received them, I felt this huge appreciation that someone would go out of their way to connect like that. They care enough about me to take the time to write what they felt and openly share their vulnerabilities – their fears and frustrations, their wants and needs and desires – with me.

As a result, once it popped up on my radar again I was very fast to implement the strategy I heard from Mal Emery and Steve Sims. Out of everything I've shared with you in this book, out of every single strategy I've shared with you, this has to be in the top three, potentially even the most valuable, strategy – which sounds ridiculous because, it seems like it has the least to do with business.

Either Way... The Sending of Personal Handwritten Notes is Without a Doubt the Most Personally Rewarding Strategy in This Book.

Like I've said earlier, business is really based on human connection, and the greatest way to build human connection is to reach out to humans and share who you are, share why you appreciate them, show your gratitude, show your love, your enthusiasm, your presence, and your certainty.

On the back of implementing this strategy, I have directly correlated the sending of personal notes to $100,000 in sales to my business and I have only been doing it for 6 months. It's mainly come in the way of referrals but, also, keeping the client around because I've gone out of my way to connect with them.

I recently moved to Argentina for a two-month change of scenery and I stopped sending personal handwritten notes for a little while because I told myself it was too hard. What I noticed is that I had a decrease in income. I had a decrease in referrals. I know – without a slither of a doubt – that it was because I wasn't connecting emotionally with my clients as much as I was previously. Needless to say I'm back on the 'Personal Handwritten Notes' like never before. It's one of my daily metrics in my Seed of Life Score.

You see, when I have a moment with a client, when I connect with someone and I feel it authentically within myself. I don't just leave it at that. I sit down and I give myself ten minutes, or twenty minutes, sometimes I even give myself half an hour or an hour. I sit down and I tell this person all the reasons why I appreciate them.

The honesty and authenticity I'm showing them in this moment drives our relationship so much further than if I was just to say that over the phone or if I was just to say that even in person. There is something amazing about the personal handwritten note and I would love you to just try it.

Authentically try it – that is the key to this.

You cannot want to make more money from it because that's

not how it works. You have to want to connect and add value. Wait for the moment to strike you. Sit and wait for it to come to you and say, "This is the moment."

I gave my Nanna that letter on her 80th birthday and it was way before I had started implementing this strategy in my business. It was something I felt like I wanted to do. My Nanna says that it's her favourite possession. She reads it all the time. And it's because I was so honest, open and vulnerable in a way I've never been with her before. I shared my appreciation. I shared my gratitude for all she's done in my life. Because of that, my Nanna and I have an amazing connection because there is no question about how I feel. I wasn't sitting back and hoping she'd understand. I put pen to paper.

This strategy is just so rewarding.

ACTION ITEM - Who the people are in your life and business you want to show gratitude to? Go to your favourite café. Sit down. Buy a beautiful notebook. Maybe even go and buy a beautiful pen and put *it* to paper.

SIDE NOTE; The two greatest investments of my life to date are my Montblanc pen and my Montblanc notebook. I carry them around everywhere. They do not leave my side. This is how much I value the process of mixing my neurology, psychology and physiology which is exactly what you are doing when you are physically writing. You're integrating your whole mental and physical world by writing physically with a pen. Why not enhance this process with, as Mont Blanc call them, a 'Writing Implement...' Coining original language was a close contester for a strategy in the book.

Could you do that? Could you sit down and write a heartfelt letter to your friends, to your family, and to your clients? See what the impact of this is. See what happens in your life over the next two, three, four, five weeks.

My mentor Dr John Demartini, once said to me, "When you love people for who they are, they turn into who you would love them to be." When you show your appreciation, you don't just take steps towards that; you take leaps and bounds.

STRATEGY 19 – How to BUILD Habit Forming Products

In the early 1900's, there was an advertising executive named Claude Hopkins.

Claude was one of the greatest copywriters to live and was personally responsible for developing a habit that the majority of the world still implements to this day, unknowingly. There aren't many people throughout the history of the world who can lay claim to this sort of influence.

Claude had a friend who was the owner of Pepsodent toothpaste. Their sales were slumping at that stage. In the early 1900's, very few Americans were brushing their teeth.

So Claude and his friend got together to devise a plan. What they did to reverse the sales of Pepsodent was to first find a new trigger. The reason people weren't brushing their teeth is because they hadn't formed the habit of it yet. Claude, being the brilliant man he was, came up with the strategy to build a habit-forming product.

First of all, they specifically changed the advertising material. They changed the advertising material to target beauty. They polarized people, claiming that their teeth were grimy and had plaque on them which was making them less sexually attractive. Because the human race is so driven by sex, this tapped into a deep human desire. The sales of Pepsodent toothpaste went through the roof.

In Charles Duhigg's seminal book, 'The Power of Habit', he lays out habits as a feedback cycle. First we get a trigger or a cue for the habit, then we enter into a routine, and seek a reward.

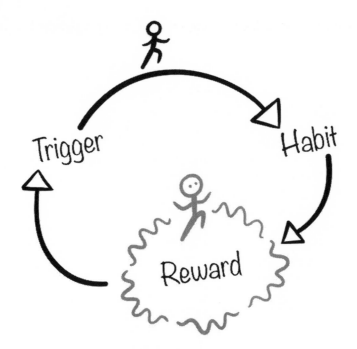

Now at Pepsodent, they had created a trigger, they had a routine, but now to create a reward for brushing the teeth that was more than just imaginary sex. Equal for all, they needed something tangible, so they inserted an ingredient into the toothpaste – and you'll probably feel this when you brush your teeth – it gives a glistening feeling – almost like your teeth are vibrating after brushing.

The ingredient serves no purpose in actually cleaning the teeth. However, it creates an unconscious reward for the habit. Therefore, they had their trigger, the routine, and we finally get the reward, which is the feedback cycle of a habit-forming product. Therefore, Claude Hopkins created a new habit within the minds of the American psyche and therefore, the whole western world. Claude has been primarily responsible for the two to three minutes we spend every day brushing our teeth.

This understanding isn't strictly limited to the mind of Claude Hopkins. It's said that 40 percent of your daily actions are habit. The largest companies in the world today are very aware of this and they've tapped into it in a way that is either quite empowering for quite shocking depending on which side of the equation you fall.

Think about Facebook. How many times do we check the Facebook feed? We get a trigger... "I wonder what my friends are thinking about." Then, we habitually pick up our phone. Then we get a reward when we see that they've liked our photo or, someone has shown emotion to us and we get the reward. Then, we start the loop again. We put our phone away for ten minutes and we bring it right back out when that thought creeps in again.

Twitter, Google – all of these platforms are the same. Whenever we have a question, we get a trigger and we habitually type it straight into Google and the reward is instant knowledge. Any time we don't know where we are, we just type it into Google Maps. Any time we want to go somewhere, we can pull out the Uber app.

All of these products have tapped into habits deep within the psyche and as a result have built the largest industries in the world off the back of understanding basic psychology.

There's a great story in Charles Duhigg's book, The Power of Habit, where he speaks of the evolution of data analytics. The analytics these sorts of companies have on us today is quite profound. It's excellent for us as business owners but, as a consumer, it can sometimes be a little bit overwhelming.

In this specific example, Target, the company, was running an advertising campaign. They had recently employed a young, up-and-coming data analyst. This data analyst realized that he could start to predict via his mathematical models, when someone was pregnant by the items they were buying in Target before the person even knew they were pregnant.

In the age of information, what we're coming to right now is a level wherein computers and mathematical models are beginning to accurately predict our own decisions, our habits and behaviour us whilst we are completely unconscious to it.

Using its huge list of resources, Target sent out advertising material for baby-styled products – prams, baby food, and clothing – within this person's pregnancy. What they saw was their sales in those areas increased dramatically.

Though… Care does need to be taken in regards to consumer analytics. Through their data analysis target had found a 17-year-old girl and, they had taken on the perspective that this girl was pregnant. They started sending brochures to this young lady's home and her father kept picking them up and reading them. He thought it was a bit strange so he went into Target and had a bit of a blow-up and said, "Well, why are you sending my daughter all this stuff about babies? She's 17 years old. She's in school. She doesn't need to be thinking about this stuff right now!"

A few months later the father apologized when the girl did turn out to be pregnant. However, this opened the door to the realization of the analysis that was going on and certainly left a few consumers feeling off-guard.

There's a great quote from Nir Eyal in his book, Hooked: How to Form Habit-Building Products. *"It is not the best product that wins but the one that holds the monopoly of mind."* This is what we need to start implementing in business. If these big companies can use it, we can use it too. Though on a lesser degree, we can still implement these sorts of strategies with our products.

ACTION ITEM - Leverage off a habit-forming product that already exists… If you don't have one already - **Start a Facebook Group for Your Clients.** 90 percent of prospects and clients will be on Facebook and you can tap into the habit formation Facebook has already spent millions of dollars on.

The cycle is already flowing – and it's one of the greatest feedback cycles that has ever existed – the cue, the routine, and the reward is happening ten, twenty, to fifty times a day. As a business owner, you can slot yourself right into this habit formation by simply running your Facebook group, and posting in it every day, whilst you build your tribe.

This is a great way to form a habit for your clients of engaging with your Business and keeping you at the top of their consciousness.

Key Takeaways From The Average Years Your Client Stays Section;
(You Fill In Here)

1. ....
....
....
....

2. ....
....
....
....

3. ....
....
....
....

4. ....
....
....
....

5. ....
....
....

Your Business History

List an experience from your past that is explained by the strategies in Sales Section.

....

....

....

....

....

....

....

....

....

....

....

....

....

....

....

....

List 5 Ideas For New Strategies to Increase the Average Years Your Client Stays;
(You Fill In Here)

1. ....

....

....

....

2. ....

....

....

....

3. ....

....

....

....

4. ....

....

....

....

5. ....

....

PROFIT MAXIMISER # 7;
REFERRALS /
CLIENT / YEAR

Did you know; if every client brings, on average, between 0 and 1 person greater than your churn rate, you are growing in a linear fashion... and if they bring more than one person, you are growing exponentially...

–Ben Slater

STRATEGY 20 – Why You Must Lead With REWARD to Drive More Referrals

Earlier on in the book, we spoke of one of the most important questions to ask in business:

"What can you afford to pay to make a sale?"

Your answer to this question can lead you into new depths because, like you've seen in the evolution of this book, it's not all about Facebook, and social media. There is a before, during and after to every sale. Once you know what you're working with you can then accurately assess the conflicting and contrasting elements you can use to drive home more sales?

BUSINESS BREAKTHROUGH QUESTION – "When thinking of referrals... What you can pay to make a sale there? Would you allocate this same amount to a referral?"

BUSINESS BREAKTHROUGH QUESTION - "How much can you allocate to any factor that is going to increase your referrals?"

One of the greatest ways to increase the amount of referrals you're going to get is to use gift boxes. When someone first becomes a client, the earlier they are presented with the opportunity to give a referral, the more likely they will be to give one. Once they give one, the floodgate may just open... Especially if you lead with rewards.

Therefore you want to put your best foot forward here. As a mentor Mal Emery taught me, lead with the 'WOW.' You want to take this person to new heights straight away and show them how committed you are to their results.

A gift box might include you sending them pillows with an accompanying note; "I'm glad you're going to be able to sleep so much better after doing this work together." It doesn't have to be something expensive. It could be something sentimental and maybe even an insider joke you had on the call. These usually work better, because they are based off unique connections.

Look at it this way... By connecting, what you're doing is marketing yes, but you're not just marketing. You're selling; you're building the relationship, building rapport, trust and value because you're connecting emotionally with your client.

Can you begin to see what I'm saying when I say people have no idea what marketing and sales really are?

One of the most multifaceted ways to grow your business is, as you've seen, to simply connect in new and unique ways. One of the best ways to connect in an emotional way is to send someone a package and make it lumpy. Lumpy means that it's a sizable package. It's got dimensions. The larger the dimensions, the more successful this will be.

There's a reason I used pillows as an example because pillows are very large and they weigh very little. Pillows would be one of the best things to send in the mail because it's going to be cost-effective. You can use a little metaphor or an idiom and make a laugh out of it, and it's going to be a large box, which is going to blow people away. It's quite a clever strategy and something that we could all use and benefit from.

As a second element to this, not just using gifts for new clients but also rewarding referrals. When you get a referral, you should reward the one who referred to you handsomely. And publicise it for the rest of your clients.

I have been known to buy people Montblanc notebooks – they're about $150 AUD – if I get a converted sale or referral and it's something that means a lot to people. It may not be something they'd go out and buy themselves, but it's a luxury item. They're going to remember me each time they sit down and use it. If it were a high-ticket sale, I would even consider buying someone a Montblanc pen and spending $500 on a pen or something of this nature. Stay tuned for an actionable example of this in the next chapter - How to run a Referral Campaign...

The more that you reward referrals, and if you're operating in your tribe, You can post into your tribe... "Hey, Jayden, just send me a referral...' Etc... and it turned into a sale so I bought him this gift to thank him for being an amazing client and doing great work to grow this tribe and grow this community." This encourages everyone else to do the same. You want to train your clients to give referrals; by firstly making it well known you accept them and secondly that they will be promptly rewarded when they do.

Most people want to give referrals but they don't because as business owners we rarely frame the right proposition. We never build the system for it and, most of the time, it's simply because we don't ask.

If you can encourage and train clients and trustees to give referrals, it is one of the greatest ways to grow your business. If you think about it this way, for every client that comes into your business, they bring at least one client with them, you never have to spend a dime on 'conventional marketing' ever again because the moment that metric becomes greater than one, your business is growing exponentially.

Again, this is why I say business owners are too fast to look externally before addressing their internal goldmine. I think this is not only a great metaphor for personal development and a great metaphor for life, but it's also very powerful in business. With a deep study and an understanding of 'The Systems For Business Philosophy' then with taking the right actions on the back of your new knowledge... You should be able to stop 'Conventional Marketing' today and continue to grow your business.

ACTION ITEM – Structure your new client – WOW Package. First set your budget. What can you afford to spend on each new client? Then create a system around welcoming new clients into your business.

STRATEGY 21 - How to Use a Gamification Campaign to Collect 65 Leads This Week in Your Business

I was speaking to my brother Drew a few weeks ago about a referral campaign he ran over at Alchemy, and I thought it was so uniquely valuable... I scheduled an interview with him to go over it in more depth for you...

If both your business sales system and your business model system are setup properly... There will be a minimum of 10 thousand dollars in increased revenue within your business over the next 14 days.

Drew Slater ▶ TELOS MASTERMIND ⌄
February 1 · 🔝

COMPETITION TIME ...

Cause we know you guys HATE competition ...

We would love you to fill out some honest feedback for Alchemy Institute

Your feedback and survey responses are really important to us
We want you to take it seriously

HOW TO PLAY ?

To be eligible for first prize, all you need to do is complete the survey and leave at least one referral

The winner will be drawn out of a hat next Wednesday Afternoon at 5.00 pm

Obviously each additional referral increases your chances of winning

Here is the link to the survey and feedback from

FIRST PRIZE $1000
Montblanc Pen
Private dinner *for you and a friend with Drew & Mads*

WINNER DRAWN: WEDNESDAY 7TH FEBRUARY

BEN: Drew, we were having a chat a few weeks ago and you mentioned a referral campaign involving a Montblanc pen. This immediately sparked my interest. Can you tell us a little bit about it and how it went?

DREW: Yeah. So, every three to four months, I run a strategy referral campaign. It's actually a feedback form. And what I realized is that, if I gamify it and turn it into something where people have an opportunity to win, they would be more inclined to give advice and also be more inclined to provide me high-quality referrals.

So I send out a feedback survey with some basic questions about how we can be better at Alchemy Institute, and then I say, if you want to go into the running to win a Montblanc pen and a dinner at a five-star restaurant in Sydney with me and my partner, for your partner and yourself, all you have to do is leave at least one referral – a referral by way of name, email and phone number – and I leave an unlimited number of spaces there for them to do that.

Basically, what happens then is I release that on a Monday morning and I draw the winners out of the hat. Officially, there's only first prize. But, when I draw the winners... I do a Facebook live stream video into my Facebook Group and I also award a bonus second and third prize place, which receives a Montblanc Notebook as well. I announce it live With the video in the group and all the clients tune in and watch as we pull stuff out of the hat and pick first, second, and third.

BEN: So, the prize in terms of the Montblanc has nothing to do if the referral turns into a sale. It's just a referral in the first place.

DREW: Yeah, the only caveat is; they have to let their referred person or people know we're going to get in contact. We call all of those referrals within that week and we offer them a complimentary business breakthrough session over the phone which is a 60-minute one-on-one phone consult with one of our team – either myself or one of the staff. If we think we can get the kind of results we've gotten their friends, we let them know and we invite them to come and attend a seminar.

BEN: So, you do it every three months?

DREW: Yeah, probably every three to four months. I haven't done this for a while. The last one was really successful. Our clients use this as well with great results.

BEN: Yeah, I like this, the first time that you said it... I thought you meant when someone became a client then you bought the referee a Montblanc pen. There's another level to this. You drive more engagement through the gamification in the Facebook group and via the Facebook Live Video. You're openly showing the rewards for the referrals and it's not just about the sale.

DREW: Yeah, it also turns into a competition, which a lot of high achieving people they want to win. It creates a huge buzz around trying to win, which is a pretty positive thing for the business if people are trying to refer you the most amount of people. One client put in ten referrals. And we also got some really good feedback about how to deliver a higher value product and a better product.

BEN: It's two-pronged. There's lots of stuff in here. And then, you're asking for the advice. It's very powerful. I mentioned earlier in the book, the Master of Influence, Robert Cialdini in his new book, Pre-Suasion, was saying, how you frame the question is really important. He mentioned a study that tested this and they found, when you ask for someone's opinion, they take a half step backwards. But, when you ask for their advice, they take a half step towards you. So, asking for the advice before you ask for the referral would drive way more referrals.

DREW: Yeah, that's the way it's working. I ask for critical feedback and I explain that them not being completely honest here doesn't help. So, they're quite open in their feedback and some of the feedback is quite critical. I feel like, if someone gives you some pretty critical feedback, they're probably more inclined to give you a referral after that. We got over 40 referrals in a week.

BEN: That's very powerful. If you were to compare this to your other streams of lead generation, would the total prize pool be less than you would have to pay for 40 leads using Conventional Direct Marketing Strategies?

DREW: If you consider I bought two $150 Notebooks, a $700 pen, and a $500 dinner, it's cost me more for these leads than normal. However, they're pretty qualified leads.

BEN: Yeah. Can you talk at all about how many sales you have made off the back of this?

DREW: I just had a quick look. It looks like we would have made five sales into varying degrees of programs. The results are a little skewed in that I also made a caveat that, if you have supplied a referral in the last month, you can include that as well because some people are like, "Oh, I referred you two clients last week. Do they not count?" So, I just said, "If you referred in the last month, you can also include those."

I backdated it a bit. So, the results are not completely cut and dry. They have to be analysed with a bit of discretion. However I don't think you can really compare it to just ordinary lead generation. It's a different style of lead generation. If someone contacts us and says, "Hey, can you give us more information about how you help people?" That's a different style of conversation to if we're reaching out to other people and saying, "Your friend who has this result reckons we can help you. Would you like a free consult?" I think it's such a different system completely.

BEN: Would you say people are more or less conducive to chat under the Referral Stream?

DREW: To chat they're probably more conducive, but it's not helpful if they just want to chat. What's interesting is I don't think these sales are any easier or harder to make than any other sale. However, I think there's a whole bunch of benefits you can't really measure, which would be community engagement, training the clients to refer more people. I think there is an immediate benefit but I think there's a much more exponential benefit into the future.

BEN: Yeah, I hear what you're saying – By people just seeing this sort of behaviour, it makes them think... "Hey... Maybe I should refer more."

DREW: We've seen referrals go up since the campaign because people are like, "Oh, well, they take referrals." But I guess there's also the caveat that, because the way the campaign runs is every referral that you leave is another entry into the drawing of the hat. Unfortunately, some clients just left a bunch of referrals that were really low quality and, that's not helpful. Referring people that are not the right fit for the business. So, next time, we'll probably have to build something in around that.

BEN: It's a very sexy possession – a Montblanc pen. In terms of a referral campaign you would be hard pressed to find something better. They probably wouldn't go out and buy that on their own.

DREW: Yeah It's unlikely. I took the client who won out to the store and we bought it together and it was a really good experience. I got a photo of it, posted it in the group. People are pretty pumped up.

BEN: By giving away the Montblanc pen as opposed to giving away $700 cash, do you think there's a benefit there in the Montblanc pen?

DREW: Yeah. For me, I think so. The experience of getting to spend time with me and going and buying it and all that sort of stuff I think is what they actually want. And to be seen as the person who won. It's way cooler than giving them cash.

BEN: You mentioned earlier that other people have run similar campaigns. Have they had similar levels of success with it?

DREW: Yeah, I think the most leads that I've seen generated from this campaign were about 65. And there have been varying degrees of success amongst these. Some people have converted a bunch of clients; some people have done poorly. I think you could more or less leave that variable down to their ability to sell.

There's a whole bunch of other considerations too. The back-end offer on the phone needs to be sensible. To be honest, you can't treat a referral necessarily the same way you might treat someone that's just coming off the street. You've got to have that level of nurture to your existing client but you've also got to have that level of assertiveness to the new client. There's a fine line there.

You can't bend your process for a referral. I just think there needs to be a strategy on boarding process for these guys. So, instead of putting these guys into a $36,000 or $20,000 program off the bat, a lot of them came into a mid-ticket workshop, which was a more gentle approach to jump on board and feel things out. Saying that though, there are some people who just went straight into the program because it was the sensible decision.

BEN: There's a huge amount of value in this, Thanks Drew.

DREW: No Worries.

PROFIT MAXIMISER # 8; REFERRALS CONVERSION RATES %

Referrals should be more qualified leads and therefore should close at a higher percentage. If this is not the case… You will want to restructure your systems and become much clearer in communicating who you are looking for.

–Ben Slater

STRATEGY 22 - When to Splinter Off Referral Leads Into New Streams

On conversion rates for referrals, what you should typically see is your conversion rate should be much higher. It should be ten to twenty percent higher for a referral than for a general lead.

The reason for this is you are borrowing trust of another person and, as you know, trust is the most important asset in business. This will get your foot in the door. This whole system is designed around building trust through emotional connections, through contact, through gifts, hand-written letters, everything I've mentioned in here. It's about elevating the trust.

Thinking you're operating from this elevated level, that's where you'll get the results.

Thinking about conversion percentages for referrals, you don't want to bend your system for anybody. One mistake I have personally made in the past is acquiring referrals that weren't qualified. I had skipped my education-based marketing stages, because I didn't have the right assets available to me. I therefore moved straight into the selling environment.

I was borrowing trust, yes, but you still want to elevate that level of trust a little bit higher. Secondly you want to make sure this person is pre-interested, predisposed, and pre-qualified to do business with you.

Let me explain an example...

I've got a chiropractor client. He has a friend who wants to get into a new business. I'm a business coach and a consultant so he says, "Hey! Why don't you go and speak to Ben? He's going to be able to help you out." Now, I don't know anything about this guy's situation. I don't know what business he's trying to get into; I'm going in blind. Am I going to be able to help him? Yes. Is he going to like it? Under the strategy of pre-eminence... Maybe not?

By the way this was before I was exclusively working with only established businesses that are making at least $750 per client in their lifetime value. Anyway this client sends over his friend. We spoke on the phone, we had a conversation, and I ended up telling him the truth. What he was trying to do was very noble and passionate but his strategy wasn't great. He should consider doing it in a myriad of other ways I then went on to suggest.

As a salesperson and as a business coach, I have to do that. It's my job. I can't bullshit someone around their idea. There is quality of life at stake here... I have to say it like it is. I have to run the strategy of pre-eminence. Otherwise, I'm not serving this person and I'm not helping them.

Now, the issue with this is that he was very attached to his own ideas and he then went back to the old client and complained, "Oh, well, this guy is a jerk and he said all these things to me," which at some degree could have been true but I have a saying in life. "Everyone gets what they need." He would have lost a lot of money so the truth was warranted.

However because this person wasn't pre-interested, pre-qualified or pre-disposed to talk to me I ended up wasting a bit of my time, though I was able to help him – which was really nice. But what would have been better is if I had plugged this person into a separate referral campaign – a separate strategy designed to either qualify or disqualify him.

For example, the reason I started writing this book was to use this as my referral strategy. This is the bed I sleep on in my businesses. This book you are holding in your hands right now, every single one of these strategies, I have implemented and currently implement across my businesses. It is literally 'The Systems For Business Philosophy.' This is my business plan. I don't follow the accounting numbers. I employ someone for this because I am not equipped to handle the accounts.

I focus on the lifetime value numbers. I focus on what's happening with lead generation, sales conversions, with average dollar sales, with churn and with referrals. I focus on the strategies that I'm implementing that month to increase those numbers.

So my first thought when I built this system for myself and

started using it - was that under Profit Maximiser 8 - How to increase referral conversion rates – was to write this book and give it to my clients to give people who may be interested in doing business with me, before they spoke with me.

Whenever someone gave me a referral, I was going to give him or her back this book and say, "Tell the person to go and read this. If they qualify, if they're pre-interested, if they're pre-disposed and if they're then available to do business with me, tell them to call me." I don't have the time to just speak to just anyone on the phone anymore. My time has become more valuable.

This is the problem you'll get with referrals. Because they come in through a different channel, it's not as controlled by you. You don't own it. So, you need to re-own it...

As you can tell, you're holding this book in your hands.

What happened was, as I finished writing this book, I started to realize I should release it to the public. I originally thought the book was going to be too valuable to give away to the public. You probably may even have got this in your hands for free, or just paid shipping and handling.

But I thought, "You know what? Why keep this information behind the curtain? Why don't I show you what you and your business can do?" Because these strategies are a small percentage of the strategies I've got in my toolkit and it's continuously growing.

I have a belief that the only people who are scared to share their ideas today are the ones who will be coming last in the acquisition of new ones tomorrow.

So, I decided to launch it as a give away.

Key Takeaways From The Referrals Section;
(You Fill In Here)

1. ....
....
....
....

2. ....
....
....
....

3. ....
....
....
....

4. ....
....
....
....

5. ....
....
....

Your Business History

List an experience from your past that is explained by the strategies in the Referrals Section.

....

....

....

....

....

....

....

....

....

....

....

....

....

....

....

....

List 5 Ideas For New Strategies to Increase Your Referral Conversion Rates;
(You Fill In Here)

1. ....

....

....

....

2. ....

....

....

....

3. ....

....

....

....

4. ....

....

....

....

5. ....

....

PART 3:
3 STRATEGIES FOR OFFERS AND CONVERSION

In this section of the book we will be tying everything together into a whole...

To build your conversion systems you must present offers that are a match to the right market. Nothing will shoot down your business faster than presenting the wrong offers to people who don't know you and don't trust you.

There needs to be a process of warmth...

You can't bring the water to boil with a snap of your fingers; it's a spectrum, a process.

THE SALES SPECTRUM

COLD   WARM   HOT

The reason why I've split these chapters up towards the end

here is because I didn't want to show you how to fill up a bucket with holes in it.

In the chapters to follow, we're going to focus on getting your offers right to build trust with your audience, then we're going to look at conversion and how you can turn people who don't know you into customers and then into clients.

Another reason why I've finished the book with these chapters is because I needed to present you with the philosophy so far. To understand funnels you need to understand education-based marketing. You need to understand storytelling. You needed to understand the dream client.

Had I presented this system at the start of the book, it wouldn't have made any sense.

These final three strategies here are direct response lead generation and sales strategies.

Also, something to consider: the strategies I've shared with you in the book are intended to be evergreen – meaning that they're going to work continuously. You could be reading this book today or in 20 years and they should still apply. Unless human psychology changes – which is highly, highly unlikely – these strategies aren't going to change.

This being the case, I have decided to leave out tactics and stick clearly to strategies only... With a little research and some testing you will easily be able to find the current tactics of the day...

I'm sure you could find more about those here; www.thesystemsforbusiness.com

So let's have a look at how it's done.

Strategy 23 – The MARKETING LADDER

In this chapter you will uncover the 3 separate segments that require three separate offers in your business... You will want to build a marketing ladder that ascends people through this platform from cold to hot.

COLD Traffic – Don't Know You, Don't Trust You

WARM Traffic – Know You, Don't Trust You

HOT Traffic – Know You, Trust You

It becomes important to note... All elements of the marketing ladder are FREE! The first goal of business is to generate an email address and name. From there we ask for their time, then during the warm or the hot offer you can ask for the order.

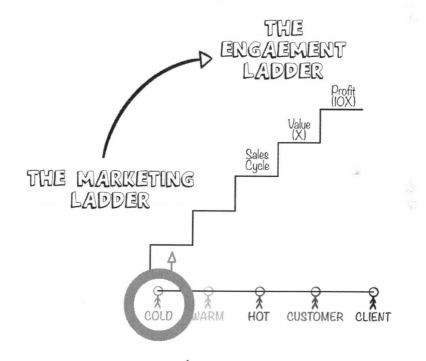

The Cold Offer

Goal – The Email Address

Specs – Short Actionable Advice Consumed in Under 5 Minutes
Examples – Cheat Sheets, Guides, Reports

There are two major variables you will want to address when marketing to people who don't know you and don't trust you...

1. HIGH SPEED

If I had never met you before and I walked up to you in the middle of the street and asked you for 45 minutes of your time what would you say to me?

This is why this book is not a cold traffic offer... It's a warm/hot traffic offer. Also the book is not free. Though if it was, someone would still have to read it for roughly 4 hours or more...

Remember that people are lazy and they want a quick fix... They want to learn now. The more you appeal to these wants and needs in your marketing, the more successful your list building and cold offers will become.

2. HIGH VALUE

Secondly you will want to present as much value as possible to your prospects in this short opt in. Think about their pain points... What are they struggling with at the moment?

How can you help to remove those pains?

And in the delivery don't hold anything back here because you think it's too valuable... That's scarcity thinking that won't see you go to the next level.

The entrepreneurs who truly succeed in marketing are those who consistently give away their best information for free and charge for implementation.

Go back to your Dream Client Profile and look into their psychographics.

Earlier in the book I said;

"You have to enter in through their emotional filters... **What are their fears, frustrations, wants, needs and desires?** You can't simply produce rational messages because these messages will forever keep your business limited at steady, stagnant, and expected straight lines."

THE COLD OFFER CONTINUUM

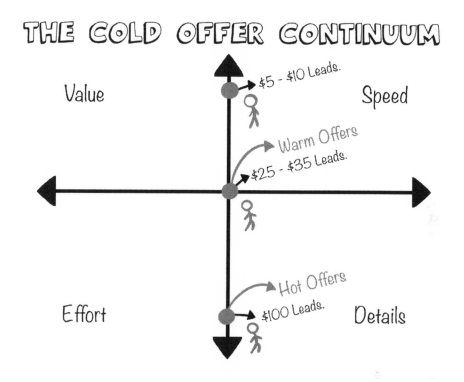

A Cold Offer should be low effort (easy to consume), low details (email only), high speed, and high value.

Here's what ends up happening if you get this wrong...

If you market Hot Offers to Cold Traffic you will be getting leads for $100 +, if your lucky

If you market Warm Offers to Cold Traffic you will be getting leads for about $25 - $35

If you market Cold Offers to Cold Traffic you will be getting leads for about $5 - $10

After your prospects have consumed your cold offer, you will want to present your warm offer. This can be done by a variety of channels, which are likely to change at some stage in the future. However most basically, you could follow up with an email sequence or an online advertisement to get your prospects into your warm offer.

Warm Offers

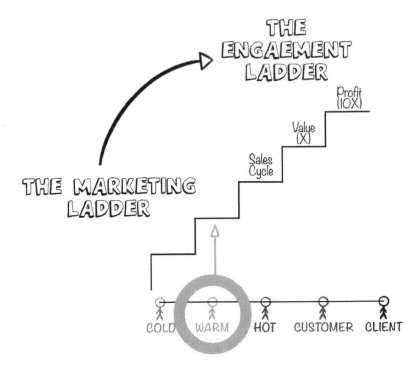

Goal – Time Commitment, Building Trust,

Specs – Presentation, 45 - 75 Minutes to Consume

Examples – Live Webinar, Automated Webinar, Video Training Series

Once someone knows who you are, it becomes much easier to ascend this person onto a webinar or something that requires a little more time, effort and details to get involved.

With the warm offer you will want to do educate your prospects but also sell yourself at the same time. The best way to do this in my opinion is a live webinar; because you can interact with your prospects, deliver huge value, lace with social proof and present offers at the end as well.

A great way to structure this is to keep to a weekly schedule... Do a weekly webinar to ascend the weekly members of your cold offer onto your video training.

HOT OFFERS

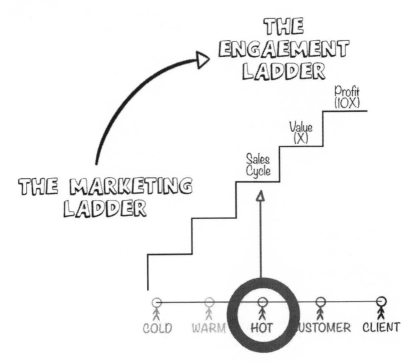

Goal – The Order

Specs – Solving Problems, Asking For the Credit Card Details

Examples – Application Phone Call

Depending on what sort of business you run you will or won't need a Hot Offer in your business... If your first product or service is less than $1000 you would be best selling your product off the back of your webinar and achieving great leverage in the process...

However if your first product or service is greater than $1000 you would likely be best taking an application phone call at the end of your webinar or video training presentation.

See Strategy 25 for the Client Application Script you can adapt, and use for this inside your business...

ACTION ITEM – BUILD YOUR MARKETING LADDER BELOW

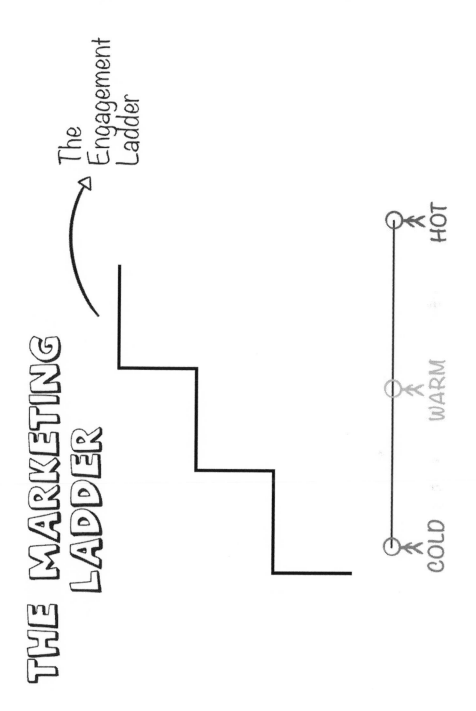

Do You Have Customers or Clients?

Why do you go to the same place for coffee every morning?

As I sit here writing this in a Cafe in Buenos Aires... My barista Diego comes to mind, from the moment I first walked in here, I faced two issues. I had been unable to find a good coffee in this city, so I was getting a little bit antsy, and I was unable to speak the language so even purchasing a coffee was hard for me.

But Diego was different. From the moment I met him, I knew I wanted to come back. He treated me like a client and friend, he did speak my language which put him at a distinct advantage, but he used it well, he sat with me and spoke about the coffee, what to do in the city, and about my work.

He was smart.

And as a result I went back there everyday for a few weeks. Was the coffee any better? Absolutely, I rationalised that to myself many times. But was it really? Probably not...

I went back every day for 3 weeks.

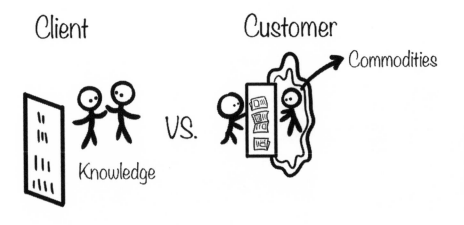

The word 'client' comes from ancient Roman roots, and was used to describe one member of the public 'Under the Protection' of another.

And most business owners have this horribly wrong. If you are only searching for customers, you will forever be a commodity destined to discounts, selling on price, and complaining about economic cycles at family barbeques.

You will have bastardised your value.

Your business must involve moving customers to clients via ways of building rare and meaningful relationships.

Why can an upper class restaurant charge 1000% more than the local Chinese takeaway? Because you are their client, you receive service and patronage.

By my definition a customer is someone who buys something from you once... A client is someone who makes continuous and repeat purchases over an extended period of time. Preferably a monthly retainer.

Why have Tesla risen to such power and notoriety in recent years? Because when you buy a Tesla you are part of their tribe. You are a client. I watched a testimonial video on their site recently and it was one the best pieces of marketing I've seen in my life.

Here's a direct quote from the video...

"When you buy a conventional car your interaction with the people who build it has ended at that point, when you buy one of these cars, your interaction has only just begun."

God, that makes me want a Tesla, and as you can see here they are notably using this powerful advantage in their business. It goes far above and beyond anything else in the market, and that's what you need to orchestrate in your business.

Jay Abraham once said, "If you truly believe that what you have is useful and valuable to your clients, then you have a moral obligation to try to serve them in every way possible."

This book has been all all about how you can optimise the relationships you share with your customers and your clients. As you do this you will notice your business has little to do with your products and services, and more to do with how you make your prospects and clients feel.

When you master this you help them to grow under your protection, and as they do, you both make a return on investment, and have a lot more fun.

Let's have a look at the best way I've found to turn customers into long term clients.

STRATEGY 24 - Creating Customers Through Events and Seminars

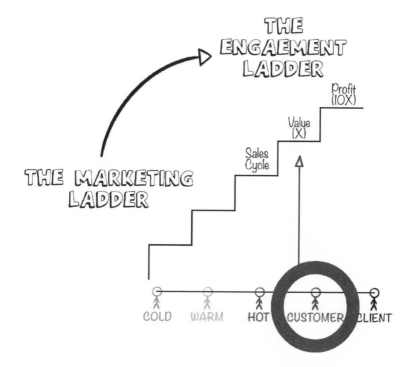

Goal – Hand pick top performers to become clients

Specs – 1 – 10 Day Event

Examples – The Seed of Life Event, Systems For Business Live

If someone is going to buy something from you once, why not make it the most emotional, trust building, and value enhancing experience possible. This way you ensure a higher chance of in turning a one time purchase, into a meaningful relationship, and then into a client.

You have put yourself in the best position to take the next steps.

In my experience, there is no better way to generate clients, than to run events. You just can't get the same levels of value, information, and screening of prospective clients, at scale, through any other channel.

I will go on record to say there is no better way to build an Intellectual Property based business than by running paid events...

How to Structure Your Event...

Over the past 5 years I have participated in close to 50 events across the areas of Personal Development, Wealth, Health and Business... I have also hosted and run 7 day retreats, afternoon events, 50 person seminars, and 3 person master classes.

I have attended, hosted, and participated in seminars on many levels of the spectrum, and without tooting my own horn; it's what I do best in business.

The only reason being, I have attended so many, and been able to build my own system around it.

Business Breakthrough Question – What is the most important and valuable piece of knowledge you could serve your prospective clients with? What is the most important and valuable breakthrough you have ever had in your life?

Structure your event around this.

What's quite interesting about the Marketing Ladder and the Engagement Ladder is that the knowledge contained within, is the same throughout all levels... However the level of engagement, and the implementation of the ideas, rises at each level.

Teach the same knowledge at your event that you would to your clients... Let them try before they buy. You will generate huge numbers of clients off the back end of the event if you hold nothing back.

During events I like to teach in a harmonious format, to do this you have to use the left and right brain, you have to appeal to the different modalities in the room... You have to help your customers intellectualise but also experience your lessons...

THE BREAKTHROUGH MODEL

I. What's the primary question?

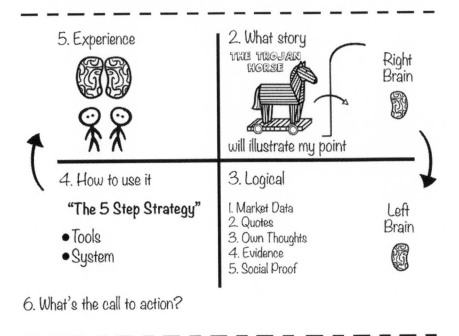

5. Experience

2. What story

THE TROJAN HORSE

Right Brain

will illustrate my point

4. How to use it

"The 5 Step Strategy"

- Tools
- System

3. Logical

I. Market Data
2. Quotes
3. Own Thoughts
4. Evidence
5. Social Proof

Left Brain

6. What's the call to action?

This is the way I like to do this at events...

1. Pose Questions

At events I will typically start by getting the audience to ask questions about themselves or to test themselves on what they will be learning throughout the day. There is nothing better for learning and receptivity to more fully understand your own ignorance.

You can also use questions to build desire...

Business Breakthrough Question - What is the primary question you want to answer in the minds of your customers?

2. Start With Stories – Right Brain

When I teach I try to start every major point with a story to illustrate what I'm trying to say. By doing so I am presenting a right, and then a left brained perspective, aimed at the same goal. Always enter in through the right.

Use the Trojan Horse.

Questions to Ask: A scrupulous teacher, in every message he communicates, will ask at least four questions, "thus: 1. What am I trying to say? 2. What Words will express it? 3. What image or idiom will make it clearer? 4. Is this image fresh enough to have an effect?"

3. Logic – Left Brain

I then present my own intellectual thoughts or any facts, stats or market data. This way you can Blitzkrieg your room... In a loving way of course.

Question to Ask: Are there any relevant facts, quotes, statistics or data to drive home my point?

4. How to Use it...

I then take any questions and set some collaborative intentions with the group based off the new knowledge. In this section I present how to use the Knowledge. I have a rule in teaching; I never present something unless there is a measureable, consistent and systemised method of using it.

5. Experience the Learning's

We then look to action the ideas into exercises and emotional experiences so that people can feel and experience the learning's.

If you do this correctly you will create a balanced event, which people will love because you have catered to all individuals in the room.

6. Action Items:

What is the major action that will lead to the highest order of growth for your customers and prospective clients?

TAKING CLIENT APPLICATIONS AT THE END OF YOUR EVENT...

This is how simple your pitch needs to be at the end of the event:

"If you want my help implementing the ideas we have discussed today, all you have to do is fill out this short application form and we can have a chat within the next couple of days to see if you are a good fit"

In my businesses I average about 20% of event attendees becoming clients, and you can too if you structure things in the right way.

Action Item – Schedule your first event for 60 days time, this will give you enough time to get your marketing sorted for the event. Run a webinar to your existing list, take strategic partnerships and start building your cold offer for the next 30 days before you get those prospects onto your webinar. Set a goal for how many bums on seats you want at your event, and get to work.

STRATEGY 25 - 'THE 5 STEP CLIENT APPLICATION SCRIPT'

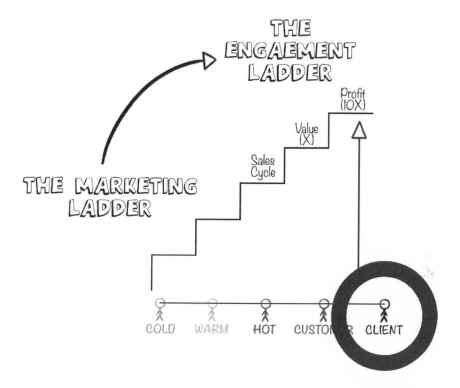

GOAL - Sign New Customers and Clients

SPECS - Prospective Customers and Clients Ask to Speak to You
Example - The Script Below

BUSINESS BREAKTHROUGH QUESTION - What is your System For Sales?

A great mentor once told me, *"People don't break; systems do."*

And you may not have a system right now... You may not be using a script. But, as a business owner, this is one of the most important things you need to be focusing on.

You need to develop your assets. And the most valuable and directly income producing asset in your business is your Client

Application Script. Remember you are auditioning the client. They have to prove they should come into your business. Not the other way around.

As we've spoken about in the previous sections on lead generation, you need to develop an asset for your education-based marketing. One that is bigger, better and going to bring you a pre-interested, prequalified, and predisposed contact detail.

Now that you know how to ascend those details onto webinars and events... It becomes important to mention that you should never make outbound calls.

You should only speak to clients who have asked to speak to you. If you are making outbound calls your marketing process is broken.

In this chapter, I'm going to teach you how to build your system to take inbound calls from prospective clients.

I can provide you with the scaffold, but you need to climb it, and start building your own structure...

Another mentor once said to me, "The quality of your life is determined by the quality of questions that you ask." John was talking about how to shift your perceptions to create the life you want. And to apply this to sales I could say...

Your ability to make sales is determined by the quality of questions you ask...

Socrates, potentially the most powerful probing mind who ever graced us once said, "I cannot make anybody do anything. I can only make them think." Socrates was so good at asking questions there is a philosophic study dedicated to his method called 'Socratic Questioning.'

One of the most important realisations to have in sales is;

Within one single question lies the power to change someone's life...

Unfortunately most people never figure this out because they have repressions around sales and money. If there is one area of life (bar spirituality) with the greatest misconceptions about what is really going on behind those closed doors. It's sales.

I know this because I was guilty of this myself.

Firstly we need to address 'The Power of Words' because this is the only thing that has ever changed the world. The person with the greatest power of words wins.

The person with the greatest power of communication wins.

There is no single philosophy that will serve you more in business than learning how to communicate effectively.

I'll take you back to Dan Sullivan's quote on selling: "Selling is getting people intellectually engaged in **a future result that's good for them** and getting them to emotionally commit to the actions that would be required for them to get that result."

Keep this in mind as you go through...

In my 'Systems For Business Client Application Philosophy,' there are 'Five Sections of the Sale.' And each of these sections is designed to build value and move onto the next.

To properly run this system you need to be spending at least 45 minutes on these conversations. There is no reason to rush it. You need to find out exactly where the person is in their life. Then, you need to understand exactly where they want to go.

At this stage, you haven't even spoken about how you can help. It's important to only ever pitch your prospects once you have made a judgement. You must be certain you can help.

One of the big mishaps I see in sales. People try to sell, far too soon... And they do it without permission too.

PERMISSION BASED SELLING

It becomes important to understand a key concept coined by my brother Drew, called 'Permission Based Selling,' After each of the 5 sections of your script you will want to ask a very important yes or no question...

BUSINESS BREAKTHROUGH QUESTION - *"Is that ok?"*

By asking this simple question, you give the prospect the permission to opt-in or opt-out... You also increase the pre-eminence in your system by doing so. If, at any time, they opt-out, they were never going to become a client and you have just saved yourself 30 minutes. And by asking their permission to move forwards, you have built authenticity and trust.

This is a completely new paradigm when it comes to sales. It is so powerful because you're not trying to sell anything.

You're adding value, which is the real key to this whole system.

STEP 1 - THE Frame

In the frame you will want to just pre-frame how the conversation will be structured. Remind the prospect why you are on the phone today and the objective of the call.

Here's a basic frame...

"Hey (NAME) so obviously you have applied to become a client and to see if you're a good fit I need to understand exactly where you're at in the business right now and also exactly where you want to go. This should take about 45 mintues.

If I can help in any way on the call that's great but If I can't that's cool too...

If I am absolutely certain I can help I will talk a bit about how you can get involved.

So, I'm going to get straight into it, *is that okay?"*

STEP 2 - THE PROBE
The goal of the Probe is to grow the conversation...

I'm trained in neuro-linguistic programming and the greatest thing I got out of that study was the power of questions, and the use of chunking...

When we're thinking about a conversation, I like to think about it as a straight line – it starts as a 2D plane. It's your job to take it from a linear 2 dimensions, into a geometric 3 dimensional organism.

To begin I will ask someone an open-ended question such as *"tell me a little bit about your story."*

It is your job to find where they're polarized – to find where they are either struggling or where they are really killing it – and understand why that is.

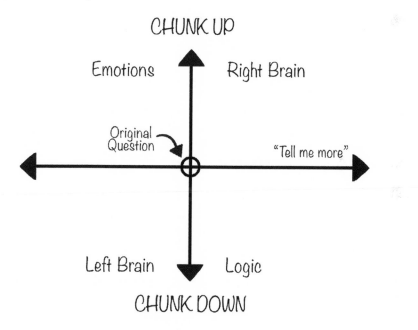

When someone gives you an answer, it is your job to probe, to find out more... Rather than shying away from their weak spot, and telling them they don't have to talk about it..

Here is how to use chunking...

1. Chunk up - move into the emotions (right side of the brain)

"Okay, and how does that make you feel?"

2. To stay on the same line of thinking (same neural pathways)

"Can you tell me a little bit more about that?"

3. Chunk Down - move down into the rational and logical (left side of the brain)

"What makes you say that?" or "Can you give me a few examples of that?"

As you can see, this is a spectrum where I can grow the conversation and I'm expanding it in all these different directions. I can ask one question and then expand it three or four different ways via this chunking mechanism.

Your client application script, is an organism. It needs to be free to move and find shape but it also must have a structure. You need to be able to go off that structure and come back to the structure. Don't be so rigid.

It's a scaffold. But it's one of those Chinese bamboo ones.

At 'Systems For Business,' I work specifically in the wealth area. So my probing questions are densely concentrated in this area. Your script may be arranged more specifically around health or relationships...

Within my different businesses, I touch on all of those areas. So each different business has a separate scripting process and a separate probing process. My questions are based on the information I need to make a judgment on whether this person is right for my products and services.

All of my scripts have the same 5 sections, however the themes of my questions will move and shift inside.

ACTION ITEM - Create headlines for your probe. What are those areas? For me, headline number one is 'business'. I need to understand everything about the business.

I need to understand 'lifetime value'.

Are you doing any 'direct marketing?'

I need to understand what your 'sales process' is.

I need to understand exactly where you are in the business right now.

What are your 'expenses'?

I need to understand 'how much money is in your business bank account right now'.

My second headline... I always touch on the 'personal life'.

No matter if I'm selling the most rational product in the world, I will still touch on what is happening in your personal life. For this, I use my system, The Seed of Life.

Remember we don't buy for rational reasons; we buy for emotional reasons and justify it rationally...

I ask questions across the seven areas of life – health, social, family, personal finance, I need to understand exactly how much money they have in the bank and in their savings, business, and career. Then ask if they are happy with their business direction right now.

Are they on purpose?

How do they feel mentally?

Coming towards the end of the probe I have understood just about everything there is to understand about this person.

Do you think anyone shows up like this on the phone?

Do you think these prospects have ever had a conversation like this before?

I get told this every single day – "this is the most amazing and interesting conversation I've ever had in my life."

And guess what? All I'm doing is asking them great questions. This is it – the power of questions raises your authority. People think that, by getting up there, you have to share. "Oh, this is what I do and these are the specs of my product, and if you would wait a minute I'll read you my brochure"

No one cares.

The only way to build authority is by asking fantastic questions. By truly understanding where your prospects are at in their life and providing them with actionable advice.

Within the probe, simply create your relevant headlines. As a tip; You must go into the personal. Otherwise, you'll never find out just how much of a master of sales you could have become.

At the end of the probing section, I ask, "Okay, that's awesome. I understand exactly where you're at in your life right now, but I need to understand where you want to go. Is that all good?"

STEP 3 – BUILDING THE PICTURE OF THE FUTURE

Now, the third section of the script is what I call 'Building the Picture of the Future.'

For this, I use a very specific question:

BUSINESS BREAKTHROUGH QUESTION - "(NAME,) I'd like you to imagine it's twelve months' time, you have become a client. And in that time, you've set and achieved all of your goals. In twelve months' time, what are you and I celebrating?"

In that moment, the person will give you the outcome that they're looking for in relation to the coaching or in relation to the education you're giving in the area of life you are serving them in.

They will give you the perfect case scenario of what they are looking for.

In this moment, you will see whether or not this person is a right fit for your business...

If your business is designed around doubling the net profits of a business and the person says, "Look, I'm just trying to grow the business by 10 percent over the next 24 months," in that stage, I'd say...

"Well, it's probably not the right relationship for me to get into. I need someone with more drive. I need someone who has bigger goals."

It's very important to honour your process.

Also it's important to understand the goals beyond just purely financial.

You will want to understand where they want to be in their relationships. Where do they want to be in their health? Where do they want to be in their wealth?

To finish off 'The Picture of the Future' I ask...

"Ok so John, I have a good understanding of where you are in your life... I also understand exactly where you want to go. Based off what you've just told me, I'm certain we can help out. What I'm going to do now is take you through a little bit of process and show you how we can help. Is that okay?"

STEP 4 – THE STRATEGIC BREAKTHROUGHS

Strategic breakthroughs are based on your coaching process. Normally, when someone comes to you, you are providing them with some kind of breakthrough. If you're selling information, if you're selling knowledge, then this is all you sell.

Whether you know it or not, the more breakthroughs you give people, the greater success you are going to have in business.

During this stage you are showing the client exactly what you will be working on together. Then you simply ask if they want your help with the implementation.

BUSINESS BREAKTHROUGH QUESTION – What are 3 predominant beliefs, thoughts, actions or inactions that are severely holding back your dream clients? How can you reframe them?

These are what you base your breakthroughs around.

You line them up – one, two, three – and you work through those breakthroughs on the call. You aim to give them a breakthrough – to show them what they could be doing with their health, their wealth or their relationships.

Unfortunately it's impossible for me to figure out what your breakthroughs should be unless I know everything about where you are right now in your business, and I know everything about where you want to go in your business.

As part of my Systems for Business Experience – the staple event I run – we work on developing these sorts of assets. I can give you the bare bones of it. I can give you the structure. But I can't right now tell you exactly what they should be...

It's up to you to strategically test a variety of different breakthroughs to see what works for you.

And once you've worked through those breakthroughs, you will come to the most important question in the whole process...

BUSINESS BREAKTHROUGH QUESTIONS - "Do you want my help with this?"

I think this is the most important question in the whole script because the person either goes, "You know what? Yeah, I do want your help with it," or they say, "Look, it's not right for me right now."

And that's fine too, as long as you protect your precious energy.

STEP 5 – THE PITCH

Only once the person has said "yes... I want your help," you can tell them how they can get involved.

Can you see why so many businesses never make 10% of the sales they could be making? At this stage we are 45 minutes into the call and we haven't pitched anything.

This is the opposite of how most business owners run their sales process, which is another reason why people hate sales so much.

They never systemised it... They never realised how incorrectly they were running their process this whole time.

Throughout the whole script I am trying to close them into a yes or a no. It's a binary system.

I'm protecting my energy on that call. The whole time, I'm protecting my energy. Only if the prospect says yes, do I have permission to move into the pitch.

"Okay, awesome! Here's how we can help."

Some tips on pitching your product or service:

I would recommend never writing things down when you first start making sales. A lot of people sit there and write down all the goals and write down all the info from the probe. They're sitting there focusing so much on what they are writing and they are not even listening.

It's so important that you listen and you listen well. Don't write anything down. Use your memory. Train your memory. If there's ever a point where you do forget, clarify it. Ask the prospect.

People love the authenticity and the honesty there. You can say, "Look, I've just forgotten what you said there earlier about how you're going with your health. You mentioned something around having an injury. Can you just remind me exactly what that was?"

Every part of the sale - from stage one (the frame), stage two (the probe), stage three (building the picture of the future), stage four (strategic breakthroughs), to stage five (the pitch) - you need a system for.

The work you do in your marketing before the call and at the start of the call in the first four sections is by far the most important.

The work you do there will make or break the relationship.

Objections are not the fault of the prospect. They're your fault because your didn't qualify your prospects with your marketing.

It's a little bit more advanced but I teach my clients how to pre-handle them – by developing very specific marketing assets around money, time, information, trust, and around the partner. You can either strategically solve them or at least pre-empt them.

I guarantee you; there are the only five objections you will ever get on a call. And using the Systems For Business Philosophy you don't want to be talking to clients who can't afford your services, don't have time to implement the actions, who don't trust you, who need more information, or who need to talk to their partner.

It's a waste of time and will diminish your self image in relation to business.

ACTION ITEM – Create Your Script. Get together with your team and piece out each of the five sections of the sale on a page – five pages in total. Remember – the yes or no questions after each area.

ACTION ITEM – Connect Your Marketing Ladder to Your Engagement Ladder...

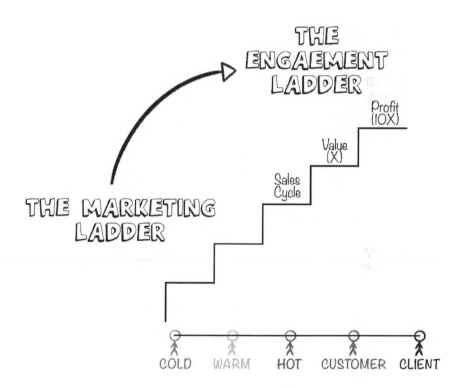

Key Takeaways From Part 3;
(You Fill In Here)

1. ....

....

....

....

2. ....

....

....

....

3. ....

....

....

....

4. ....

....

....

....

5. ....

....

....

Your Business History

List an experience from your past that is explained by the strategies in Part 3: OFFERS AND CONVERSION.

....

....

....

....

....

....

....

....

....

....

....

....

....

....

....

....

List 5 Ideas For New Strategies to Increase Your CONVERSIONS;
(You Fill In Here)

1. ....

....

....

....

2. ....

....

....

....

3. ....

....

....

....

4. ....

....

....

....

5. ....

....

ABOUT THE AUTHOR

Ben Slater is the director of two businesses, Systems For Business and The Seed of Life. He is a philosopher, business consultant, personal development mentor, speaker and educator hailing from Sydney Australia.

On the back of his ruthless pursuit into self education, he now teaches knowledge based entrepreneurs how to master their lives, grow their businesses and build personal wealth at seminars, courses, retreats and during his private consulting services. He does this through a deep understanding of psychology, human behaviour, marketing, and sales. Ben is the host of two separate podcasts, The Systems For Business Podcast and The Seed of Life Podcast.

Over the past 5 years Ben has started five separate businesses. The first was, Primal Sydney, an online bodyweight strength training program where he taught people how to handstand with his brother Drew. In this business, Ben and his brother Drew learnt how to generate leads and make sales from an online platform, and they have been teaching others ever since.

Ben then went on to start a business consulting service with his brother Drew, which grew to a $700,000 business within 12 months in 2015.

Ben will be the first to tell you his success is in direct proportion to the suffering he has been through. After dealing with mental health issues as a result of heavy drug abuse, and through the work of selfless mentors, Ben was able to find a passion for this self education you see today; and as a result it's not uncommon for him to read up to 8 books in a week...

His mission is to do everything is his power to increase the consciousness of the planet. He believes that the impact of Life changing ideas, and entrepreneurship is the most efficient path to this growth.

Systems For Business helps small businesses who are doing over 100k in sales to scale to 7 figures and beyond. To work with Ben directly in growing your business...

Head here...
www.thesystemsforbusiness.com/book-apply

Made in the USA
Middletown, DE
17 January 2020